Garth Ennis
Writer

Steve Dillon
Artist

Tom Ziuko
Colorist

Todd Klein
Gaspar Saladino
Letterers

Glenn Fabry
Original Series Covers

Warren Ellis
Introduction

JOHN CONSTANTINE, HELLBLAZER: FEAR AND LOATHING

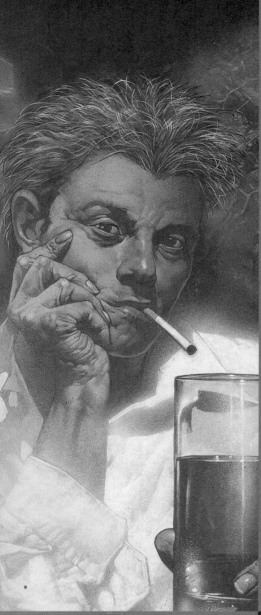

Karen Berger	VP-Executive Editor
Stuart Moore	Editor-original series
Julie Rottenberg	Assistant Editor-original series
Bob Kahan	Editor-collected edition
Axel Alonso	Consulting Editor
Robbin Brosterman	Senior Art Director
Paul Levitz	President & Publisher
Georg Brewer	VP-Design & Retail Product Development
Richard Bruning	Senior VP-Creative Director
Patrick Caldon	Senior VP-Finance & Operations
Chris Caramalis	VP-Finance
Terri Cunningham	VP-Managing Editor
Alison Gill	VP-Manufacturing
Rich Johnson	VP-Book Trade Sales
Hank Kanalz	VP-General Manager, WildStorm
Lillian Laserson	Senior VP & General Counsel
Jim Lee	Editorial Director-WildStorm
David McKillips	VP-Advertising & Custom Publishing
John Nee	VP-Business Development
Gregory Noveck	Senior VP-Creative Affairs
Cheryl Rubin	Senior VP-Brand Management
Bob Wayne	VP-Sales & Marketing

JOHN CONSTANTINE, HELLBLAZER: FEAR AND LOATHING

DC Comics, 1700 Broadway, New York, NY 10019
A Warner Bros. Entertainment Company
Printed in Canada. Fourth Printing.
ISBN: 978-1-56389-202-8

Cover illustration by Glenn Fabry.
Logo design by Nessim Higson.

This is a book about lives being ground into shit.

It's funny stuff.

I imagine a lot of you holding this book in your hands, or between your stumps or whatever, are familiar with the names Ennis and Dillon from PREACHER, which, in addition to being the best regular comic published today, is also bloody funny. This book has its funny bits, too; the piss jokes and liberal sprinklings of rabbit shit are the bad seeds of PREACHER's screaming laugh track.

The rest of you, I guess, might have flicked through this volume and are having problems with the fact that I am characterizing such things as The Death of Hope, Horrible Beatings, Disgusting Murder, Sexual Treachery, The Killing of Love and Stark Religious Horror

as funny. Tough. Garth and Steve are comfortable with these themes. It may be gallows humor, but they're at least stopping to draw a cock on the wood before they swing.

Garth Ennis is the Irishman who started writing comics in order to escape from university, characterizing the students he was locked up with as "a pack of wankers." As I write this, the bastard's just starting a month-long trip across the States with his mate Jeff, while I sit here locked in my Essex castle writing the intro for his book. It's a rough old life, being in comics. Steve Dillon has been drawing comics professionally since he was about four years old. He has about eighty-five kids and lives in Luton, because somebody has to.

"WE NEVER LIKED YOU ANYWAY."

introduction by **Warren Ellis**

This book comprises the opening shots of their collaboration. Garth had already been writing HELLBLAZER for a couple of years, taking great joy in making previous regular artist Will Simpson draw disgusting things. Will, an excellent artist, responded gamely and professionally, as he always does, but his heart was never in the horror. Will is a very nice man, and so his waking hours are not consumed with daydreams of gratuitous claret and eviscerated royalty. It was fine work, but what Steve brought to the book, in addition to his phenomenal storytelling skills (and I don't think there's a better storyteller than Steve Dillon in the monthly comic-book business right now), was an utter relish for the punished meat and torn skin. I guess that when you've worked for British publishers for as long as Steve had, you develop a higher and finer touch for these things. Garth responded in the only way he could, being Garth: he turned up the volume.

But before I get too far into that, it's worth spending a few moments with the other important character in the book: John Constantine. Frequently painted as a mystic investigator in some kind of bastardized Chandlerian tradition, Society's Knight riding against the Bad Craziness in the dark, John is one of horror fiction's more complex characters. Rather than Philip Marlowe with a magic kit, John is instead Society's Bastard, locked inside the world he hates, angry and twisted, holding a small, poisoned set of ethics to his

4

chest. And that last point is possibly the only thing that really makes him different from the rest of them. That's what makes him wake with anger and lie down with it. That little voice that says Fucking People Over Is Wrong, and No One Else Should Have To Live Like This.

In the (Christ! It's damn near a) decade since his creation, John Constantine has gone from the young English occult wideboy of Alan Moore's initial vision to the troubled and aging adrenaline addict of Jamie Delano's bleakly poetic writing, who grew crushed by the appalling weight of his own terrible life during

5

Jamie's often brilliant forty episodes. The strength of the character, that has him remain so clearly the same man even when viewed through two or three different writers' eyes, is that he is a terrific mouthpiece for anger.

Jamie's final episode of his run on the book saw John finding some kind of personal closure, having finally turned his anger inward. Once Garth got moving — and FEAR AND LOATHING really does signal Garth hitting top speed on HELLBLAZER — John Constantine, forty and fucked off, got angry with *everything*.

is grail is his girlfriend Kit."

It works because John is very clearly given things worth protecting from the world. In this piece, his anchor and his grail is his girlfriend Kit. A complex piece of work in herself, and John's superior in pretty much everything, she's another facet of the strong, intelligent woman that Garth's been writing (probably unconsciously) from his earliest work, *Troubled Souls*, to PREACHER. The world in which he wants to live with her is symbolized by the clasp of friendship, another major theme of Garth's run on HELLBLAZER and best displayed in the "party issue" contained in this book.

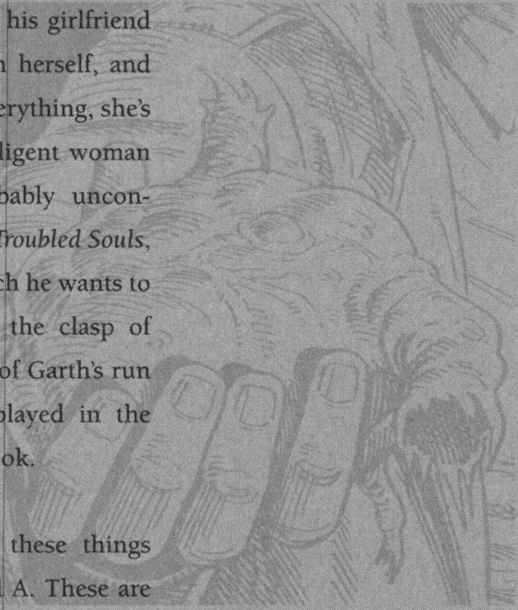

What's John protecting these things from? Authority. With the capital A. These are stories about what authority does to people, about the poison in its foundations. You can substitute Authority for Government, for the Establishment, even for God, and it all means

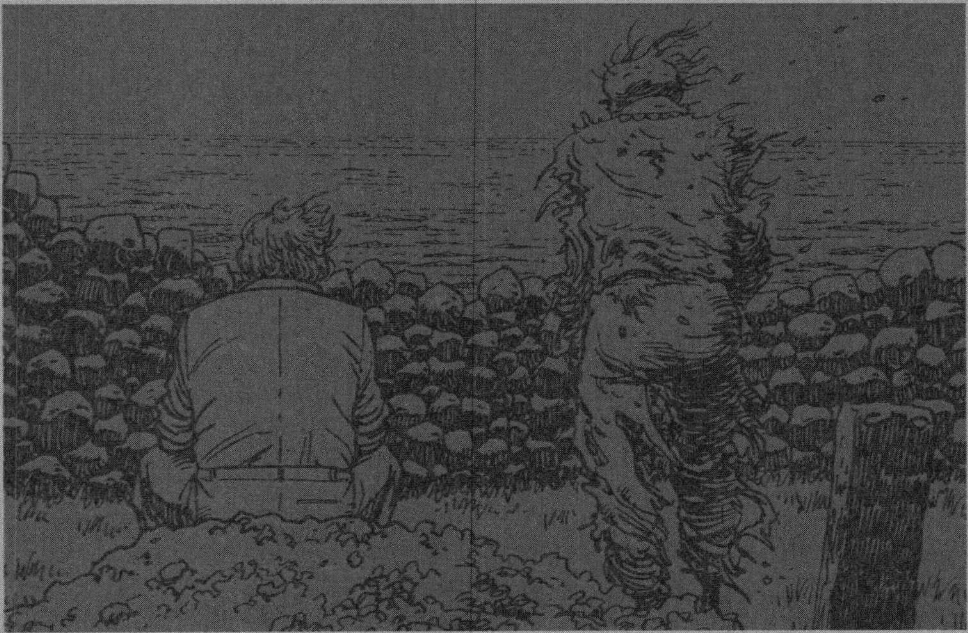

"What follows is among the very

the same thing: someone exerting control they did not earn and do not deserve, grinding lives into shit largely because they feel like it. This is where Garth and Steve found the anger, in people using our fear on us, locking us in the black iron prison of mediocrity and ignorance.

What follows is among the very best horror work of the 1990's. It retains the occult connections, but what sets it apart from the sad, played-out "dark fantasies" that you'll find on the shelf next to it is its clear knowledge that real horror is perpetrated not by eye-rolling pantomime monsters, or pale things in black with stupid names. Real horror comes only from people. Just people. They're the scariest things in the world.

Hold on, let me light up here...okay, where's the checklist? I've pretty much covered the "I know Garth, which is why I'm writing this" bit, done the quick bio bit, done the history bit and the sad litcrit bit, praised Garth and Steve to the skies so's I can get drinks out of 'em...right, I'm finished. Now go and read the sodding book.

Warren Ellis
Southend
August 1996

(Warren Ellis writes comics and tells lies for a living. His works include the wholesale butchery of the Marvel Universe in Ruins, *the politicizing and fetishizing of super-heroes in* Stormwatch *and* DV8, *and the liberal flinging-around of human meat in* Druid. *Currently preparing the political sf series* TRANSMETROPOLITAN *for Helix, Warren Ellis lives in England with his partner and daughter, and smokes a lot.)*

best horror work of the 1990's."

STEVE
DILLON

GARTH
ENNIS

CONSTANTIN

G.FABRY
15·11·92

THERE'S AN OLD GRAVEYARD SOUTH OF LIVERPOOL, WHERE THE IRISH SEA SPEWS TOXIC SHIT ACROSS A LONELY SHORE...

NO ONE COMES HERE NOW, NOT EVEN TO BE BURIED. NOTHING WAKES THE SLEEPERS, NOTHING TRAMPS ACROSS THEIR BEDS...

EXCEPT FOR NOSY BASTARDS LIKE ME, OF COURSE.

PRETTY SOON NOW I'LL FINISH THIS FAG, AND I'LL PICK UP THE SPADE...

AND THEN I'LL START DIGGING.

END OF THE LINE

GARTH ENNIS • writer **STEVE DILLON** • artist
TOM ZIUKO • colors **gaspar** • letters **STUART MOORE** • editor

IT WAS ALL SMILES AND HELLOS WHEN WE GOT TO CHERYL'S, BUT I COULD STILL FEEL THE ICE IN THE AIR...

HERE, LISTEN, CHERYL, IT'S REALLY GOOD'VE YOU TO ASK US UP...

HERE, LOOK AT THE PRINCESS!

'LO, UNCLE JOHN.

NAH, YOU'RE WELCOME ANYTIME, LUV.

HANG THEIR COATS UP, WOULD YOU, TONY?

I'LL PUT THE KETTLE ON.

I'LL GIVE YOU A HAND...

HOW ARE YOU, GEMMA?

HI, KIT.

UM...

YOU IN THE DOGHOUSE?

YEAH.

13

WHAT'S UP WITH YOU, SIS?

DON'T YOU SIS ME, SUNSHINE. WHAT'VE YOU DONE TO GEMMA?

WHAT? I ONLY JUST GOT HERE--

JOHN, I'M READY TO BLOODY WELL SMACK YOU ONE.

I HAVEN'T SEEN GEMMA FOR MONTHS... CHERYL, I THOUGHT YOU WERE HAVING US UP 'COS IT'S CHRISTMAS NEXT WEEK, NOT TO BITE ME SODDING HEAD OFF!

IS THAT RIGHT?

NOW WHAT SORT OF BADNESS'VE YOU BEEN PUTTING IN MY LITTLE GIRL'S HEAD, FOR GOD'S SAKE?

WELL, WHAT D'YOU CALL THIS, THEN?

OH, JESUS...

HERE, HOLD ON-- YOU THINK *I* GAVE HER THIS?

WHO ELSE?

BLOODY HELL, CHERYL! I'VE MESSED ME LIFE UP GOOD AND PROPER WITH THIS BOLLOCKS -- WHY WOULD I WANT TO DO THE SAME TO *GEMMA?*

SHE'S ME *NIECE...*

SHE'S MY DAUGHTER.

AW, CHERYL... I SWEAR TO GOD I DIDN'T GIVE HER THIS, OKAY? I MEAN, DID *SHE* SAY I DID?

NO. SHE WON'T TELL ME ANY- THING ABOUT IT.

D'YOU WANT ME TO HELP HER?

...AND WHEN HE CAME BACK AFTER HE SAID WE WOULDN'T SEE HIM AGAIN, I MEAN, I THOUGHT HE WAS STARTING TO SORT HIMSELF OUT...

BUT I FOUND GEMMA WITH THAT...THING, AND HE WAS THE FIRST ONE I THOUGHT OF, Y'KNOW?

AW, I DO OF COURSE, CHERYL...

BUT YOUR WEE BROTHER, YOU KNOW WHAT HE'S LIKE-- YOU AND GEMMA ARE A REAL COMFORT TO HIM. HE WOULDN'T HURT YOU IN A MILLION YEARS, LOVE.

OH, BUT YOU TOO, KIT--YOU'VE BEEN BRILLIANT FOR HIM!

er...

SO, DOES TONY KNOW ABOUT ALL THIS?

OH GOD, NO. IT'D DESTROY HIM, THE STATE HE'S IN...

SANDRA'S BEEN REALLY HORRIBLE TO ME, UNCLE JOHN. SHE NICKED BARRY OFF ME AT TINA'S PARTY AN' ALL-- AN' SHE'S MEANT TO BE ME *FRIEND!*

HE SAID HE'D PUT A CURSE ON ME.

I...I CAN'T SAY--!

AW, GEM...

SHE'S THE ONE THE PINS ARE IN ON THE PHOTO, YEAH?

GEM, WHERE'D YOU *GET* THIS?

A *CURSE*--?

WHO SAID IT, LUV? WHAT'S HIS NAME?

BECAUSE RIGHT THEN, I WANTED TO KNOW WHAT TO PUT ON THE FRIGGER'S GRAVE.

DAD'S GHOST, AND THE MAN--I MEAN, HADN'T THE KID BEEN THROUGH *ENOUGH*?

OH GOD....

ROB-ROBBIE *BROOKS.*

R.I.P.

HE'S TINA'S BROTHER. I THOUGHT HE WAS JUST A DICKHEAD, LIKE. BUT HE CAME UP TO ME WHEN I WAS ANGRY AT THE PARTY...

"HE TOLD ME HE COULD HELP ME GET BACK AT SANDRA. SHOWED ME ALL THESE BOOKS AN' EVERYTHING--IT LOOKED LIKE DEVIL WORSHIP STUFF. WITH ALL THESE STARS AN' LATIN WRITING, Y'KNOW?

"SOMEONE TOOK THE PHOTO AT THE PARTY. ROBBIE SAID IT WAS GOOD FOR THE MAGIC.

"AN' HE GAVE ME THE BOARD AN' MADE ME SWEAR NOT TO TELL.

"I WAS JUST ABOUT TO PRICK ME THUMB AND PUT BLOOD ON IT..."

AN' THEN ME MAM WALKED IN. SHE NEAR HAD A FIT.

THANK CHRIST.

'M SORRY.

S'OKAY, LUV. S'OKAY. I'LL FIX EVERYTHING UP, RIGHT?

GEM...

YOU'RE A SMART KID, LUV. WHY'D YOU WANT TO MESS ABOUT WITH THIS CRAP?

WELL...

I DUNNO... I THOUGHT I COULD GET SANDRA. I KNOW IT WAS SORT OF WICKED, LIKE...

BUT IT WAS ALSO SORT OF EXCITING, TOO.

WELL? HOW'S MY LITTLE MONSTER, THEN?

YOU'RE NOT MAD AT ME?

NO.

WELL?

SOME BASTARD'S TRYING TO GET HER INTO MAGIC.

JESUS, IT'S JUST LIKE I STARTED OUT--THEY MAKE YOU THINK IT'S THE GREATEST THING SINCE SLICED BREAD--!

I'LL HAVE TO SORT THIS WANKER OUT.

AND THEN I'LL HAVE TO PUT THE FEAR OF GOD INTO GEMMA, SO SHE STOPS IT HERE...AW, SHIT.

WHY DON'T...WHY DON'T YOU LET ME TALK TO GEMMA?

ON THE OTHER SIDE OF LIVERPOOL, AND HALF A PACKET OF SILK CUT LATER, I FOUND THE SQUAT WHERE BROOKS WAS SUPPOSED TO LIVE.

ANGER MAKES THINGS SEEM EASY. GO OUT, FIX THE BASTARD, FEEL BETTER. GO HOME.

IF ONLY.

I'M LOOKING FOR A LAD CALLED BROOKS.

SO WHAT?

OI!

PISS OFF, BOLLOCKS.

I'M NOT AFRAID OF YOU, PAL! I DO KARATE!

YOU'RE BROOKS. YOU'RE THE ONE GIVES CURSE BOARDS TO KIDS, eh?

WHAT? HAVE YOU BEEN TALKIN' TO THAT MASTERS BITCH?

SHE'S MY NIECE, YOU FAT PILE OF SHIT. WATCH IT!

YOUR--? JESUS!

JOHN CONSTANTINE! IN MY HOUSE!

OH BLOODY HELL--!

SOD OFF, BRIAN! THIS IS IMPORTANT!

THIS IS FRIGGIN' GREAT, JOHN! I'VE ALWAYS WANTED TO MEET YOU!

TERRY BUTCHER'S BEEN TELLIN' ME LOADS ABOUT YOU -- I THINK I'VE STILL GOT THE NME WITH THE MEMBRANE INTERVIEW, TOO!

COME ON AN' SEE!

I THOUGHT BUTCHER GOT EATEN, BACK-STAGE AT LIVE AID-- CHRIST, I HADN'T COUNTED ON THIS PRICK KNOWING SO MUCH ABOUT ME--

RIGHT.

YOU STUPID BASTARD. D'YOU KNOW WHAT WOULD'VE HAPPENED IF SHE'D PUT BLOOD ON THAT BOARD?

AAAAOW!

WHAT--? WH-WHY ARE YOU ANGRY WITH ME?

I MEAN, SHE'D BE DOING THE STUFF YOU DO!

WHY AREN'T YOU PROUD?!

NO, IT WASN'T GOING TO BE EASY.

IT WAS MORE THAN SOME LITTLE TURD GETTING HIS KICKS BY SCREWING UP KIDS.

I M-MEAN, WHAT'D I DO WRONG, EH?

SHUT UP. CORVUS INFERNAE. DISTRICULUM CANVANARIUS— OCULARI ARCHA DEL MALEFICUUM CARRIONDUM--

WHAT?!

THRICE BOUND.

NO! STOP!

THRICE CURSED.

NOOOOOO!

THRICE DAMNED.

OH GOD. OH NO.

OH GOD!

SACRED ARCANA. MAGUS STUFF.

YOU EVER GO NEAR GEMMA MASTERS AGAIN, ARSEHOLE, YOU'LL FIND OUT WHAT A REAL CURSE IS.

PLEEEEEASE--

NO POINT IN BEGGING, SON. YOU CAN'T REVERSE HIGH MAGIC.

GOOD ENOUGH FOR HIM, THOUGH.

NO!

PLEASE.

PLEASE.

TO BE HONEST, IT WAS JUST SOME LOAD OF SHIT I MADE UP OFF THE TOP OF MY HEAD...

PLEASE.

OH KIT, IT'S *BRILLIANT!* ARE YOU *SURE,* LIKE?

AYE, YOUR UNCLE JOHN WANTED YOU TO HAVE SOMETHING NICE FOR CHRISTMAS...

I'M TELLIN' YOU, GEMMA, YOU'RE GONNA KNOCK 'EM *DEAD* IN THAT.

THANKS.

YOU'RE DEAD GOOD TOGETHER, YOU TWO. I MEAN, JOHN NEVER REALLY LASTED WITH ANYONE BEFORE, Y'KNOW?

MM. DID YOU MEET MANY OF HIS OTHER GIRLFRIENDS?

WELL...EMMA WAS UP WITH HIM A FEW TIMES, BUT I WAS ONLY LITTLE THEN. SHE WAS NICE.

SHE WAS AYE.

SHAPES FASHION

BUT ME MAM, RIGHT-- SHE THINKS YOU'RE GREAT, SHE DOES. SHE SAYS YOU'RE UNCLE JOHN'S *LAST CHANCE.*

DOES SHE, NOW?

SOMETIMES PEOPLE ARE JUST THEMSELVES, NOT WHAT OTHER PEOPLE HOPE THEY'LL BE.

HERE, D'YOU FANCY A PIZZA?

YEAH!

I'M REALLY GLAD YOU TWO CAME, Y'KNOW. ME MAM'S BEEN *FLAMIN'* WITH ME.

AW GEMMA, YOU NEAR TERRIFIED THE LIFE OUT OF HER...

YEAH, BUT IT'S JUST THE SAME KIND OF THING UNCLE JOHN DOES, INNIT?

eh...?

JUST 'CAUSE I'M LIVING WITH JOHN, DOESN'T MEAN I LIKE WHAT HE GETS UP TO.

I WOULDN'T KNOW.

I...I THOUGHT YOU'D BE INTO IT, TOO...

NAH, BUT HE DOESN'T MIND. HE KEEPS IT AWAY FROM ME.

HE KNOWS I'M NOT INTERESTED IN THAT SIDE OF HIM ANYWAY. HE DOESN'T PUT UP A FRONT OR TRY AND BE CLEVER...

I JUST CARE ABOUT *HIM*, GEMMA.

AW, THAT'S REALLY NICE. YOU MUST KNOW WHAT HE'S REALLY LIKE THEN, YEAH?

HE'S GOOD TO YOU, GEMMA. HE BRINGS YOU PRESENTS AN' ALL, AND HE HELPS YOU OUT AND TALKS TO YOU. AND WHAT-EVER IT IS THAT'S WRONG WITH HIM, HE STOPS IT HURTING YOU.

THAT'S HIM.

YEAH, I S'POSE SO...

IT'S JUST...IF THIS MAGIC IS, WELL, WRONG OR WHATEVER-- IT JUST SOUNDS REALLY WILD, Y'KNOW?

OH, AYE. JOHN'S DONE PLENTY OF WILD THINGS, GEMMA.

HE'S BEEN ALL OVER THE WORLD, HE'S SEEN INCREDIBLE STUFF, HE'S HAD THE TIME OF HIS LIFE...

DON'T YOU?

AND HE'S CAUSED A TERRIBLE, TERRIBLE LOT OF PAIN WHILE HE'S BEEN AT IT.

THAT'S WHY HE WAS WORRIED ABOUT YOU, LOVE. HE DOESN'T WANT YOU MUCKING UP YOUR LIFE THE WAY HE DID.

OH.

I'M SORRY.

I WAS SO MAD AT SANDRA, LIKE. I... I DIDN'T WANT TO LET HER GET OFF WITH IT...

JUST RIGHT, TOO.

eh?

YOU SHOULDN'T EVER TAKE SHIT OFF ANYONE, GEMMA. I NEVER DID. BUT YOU DON'T NEED MAGIC OR WHAT-EVER. GET ANGRY IF YOU WANT. CHIN THE WEE BITCH...

IS THAT WHAT YOU DID?

IT IS.

OPEN

AND LOOK WHO I ENDED UP WITH.

JUST MAKE SURE THAT PEOPLE KNOW WHO YOU ARE AND WHAT YOU'RE ABOUT, AND THAT THEY'D BETTER NOT TRY ANY OUL' CUTENESS.

27

IT'S SOMETHING IN ME I'VE ALWAYS KNOWN ABOUT, BUT NEVER HAD THE BALLS TO FACE...

A VICIOUS, TWISTED LITTLE SHIT OF A THING THAT SCRABBLES IN THE DARK AND GIGGLES TO ITSELF--IT CAN KILL A CHILD IN THE WOMB OR HURT A LITTLE GIRL JUST 'COS SHE'S THE WRONG GUY'S NIECE--

I CALL IT FATE.

SO I'VE COME HERE TO FIND AN EXPERT ON THE SUBJECT.

CHRIST...!

SHOULD'VE BROUGHT CHAS FOR THIS.

YOU CAN STOP DIGGING NOW, YOU LITTLE BASTARD.

I'M FREE.

YOU ALMOST CUT ME IN TWO WITH THAT CURSED SPADE, YOU FOOL!

I SEE THE FAMILY CHARM IS AS STRONG IN YOU AS EVER.

IT'S BEEN TWENTY YEARS, HAS IT NOT? DID YOUR LIFE TURN OUT TO BE THE MAGICAL TRIUMPH YOU EXPECTED?

TOUGH SHIT.

IT HAPPENS TO US ALL. WE GET A SNIFF OF SORCERY AND OH! WHAT PLANS WE MAKE! WE'LL SHAKE CREATION AND LEAVE NOTHING BUT SMILES AND WIT AND A REPUTATION ALL MEN ENVY!

US CONSTANTINES.

I KNEW I WASN'T THE FIRST CONSTANTINE TO DO WEIRD SHIT--A QUICK DEKKO AT THE HISTORY BOOKS TOLD ME THAT...

BUT OLD BRENDAN, ALWAYS THE SCHOLAR, FOUND ME AN ANCESTOR WHO WAS STILL ALIVE.

HARRY CONSTANTINE SERVED WITH CROMWELL IN IRELAND, AT THE DROGHEDA MASSACRE-- BUT WHERE GOD'S FRIGGING ENGLISHMAN DID IT OUT OF GOOD CHRISTIAN MADNESS, HARRY DID IT FOR THE LOOT.

AND THEN HE MET HIS MATCH IN THE RIBBON QUEEN, AND SHE CURSED THE BASTARD TO LIVE FOREVER.

THE SPELL WASN'T THAT STRONG, JUST BLOODY AMATEUR STUFF. IF SOMEONE WANTED TO, THEY COULD STILL DO HIM IN...

SO THE QUEEN PUT HIM SOMEWHERE NO ONE COULD GET TO HIM.

NO ONE DID.

NOT FOR THREE HUNDRED YEARS.

AND THEN ONE DAY, ALONG COMES THIS ARROGANT LITTLE SOD ASKING ABOUT HIS HERITAGE...HE KNOWS WHAT A SHIT HARRY IS, AND ONCE HE'S GOT HIS ANSWERS HE JUST FILLS IN THE GRAVE AGAIN.

'COS HE THINKS HE'S GONNA BE DIFFERENT.

CONSTANTINE

BUT HE'S NOT.

HE'S JOHN CONSTANTINE.

WELL? MORE GUIDANCE AND HISTORY, IS THAT WHAT YOU WANT FROM ME?

A BLOODY FINE NERVE YOU HAVE, AFTER THE LAST TIME!

LET'S GET OUT OF THIS SODDING HOLE, eh?

WHAT RIGHT HAD YOU TO SIT IN JUDGMENT OVER ME? OR HAVE YOU ENDED UP WITH BLOODLESS HANDS?

YOU'D BE THE FRIGGING FIRST!

NO. I HAVEN'T.

I STILL DON'T KNOW WHAT KIND OF FATE IT IS THAT MAKES US INTO BASTARDS. I THOUGHT I CAME CLOSE ONCE, BUT...

...I KNOW IT TRIES TO GET US ALL.

US CONSTANTINES.

BUT SOMETHING ELSE WE DO, WE ALL TRY TO *BUCK* FATE. RIGHT DOWN TO THE LAST DROP OF BLOOD, WE STRUGGLE ALL THE WAY.

STUBBORN FRIGGERS.

MAYBE IT'S ALL WE'VE GOT.

MAYBE IT IS.

...ALL COME TO A POINT OF CHOICE. I THINK YOUR NIECE HAS REACHED HERS, AND IF SHE HASN'T ALREADY TURNED FROM THE PATH OF THE DAMNED--A FEW GOOD WORDS FROM YOU SHOULD DO THE TRICK...

MM. BUT NOW THE WIND IS FRESHENING, AND THE STARS ARE SLIPPING BACK BE- TWEEN THE CLOUDS. WE'VE LET A MOMENT'S WARMTH PUT OFF DECISION'S CHILL.

I DON'T WANT TO GO BACK BELOW, JOHN, BASTARD THOUGH I AM.

YOU'RE A BASTARD ALL RIGHT, HARRY...

BUT ONE BASTARD CAN FORGIVE ANOTHER.

THINK THAT'S ALREADY SORTED, MATE...

I WANT TO REST.

WHO ELSE WILL ?

AND THERE'S JUST A TINY MURDER IN THE NIGHT.

I THOUGHT I'D BE ADMITTING MY LIFE WAS A FAILURE, WANTING TO END THE LINE...

NO.

I BUCKED FATE. I BEAT IT.

IT'S NO FAILURE TO BE THE LAST CONSTANTINE...

'COS NOW NO ONE ELSE HAS TO BE.

The End

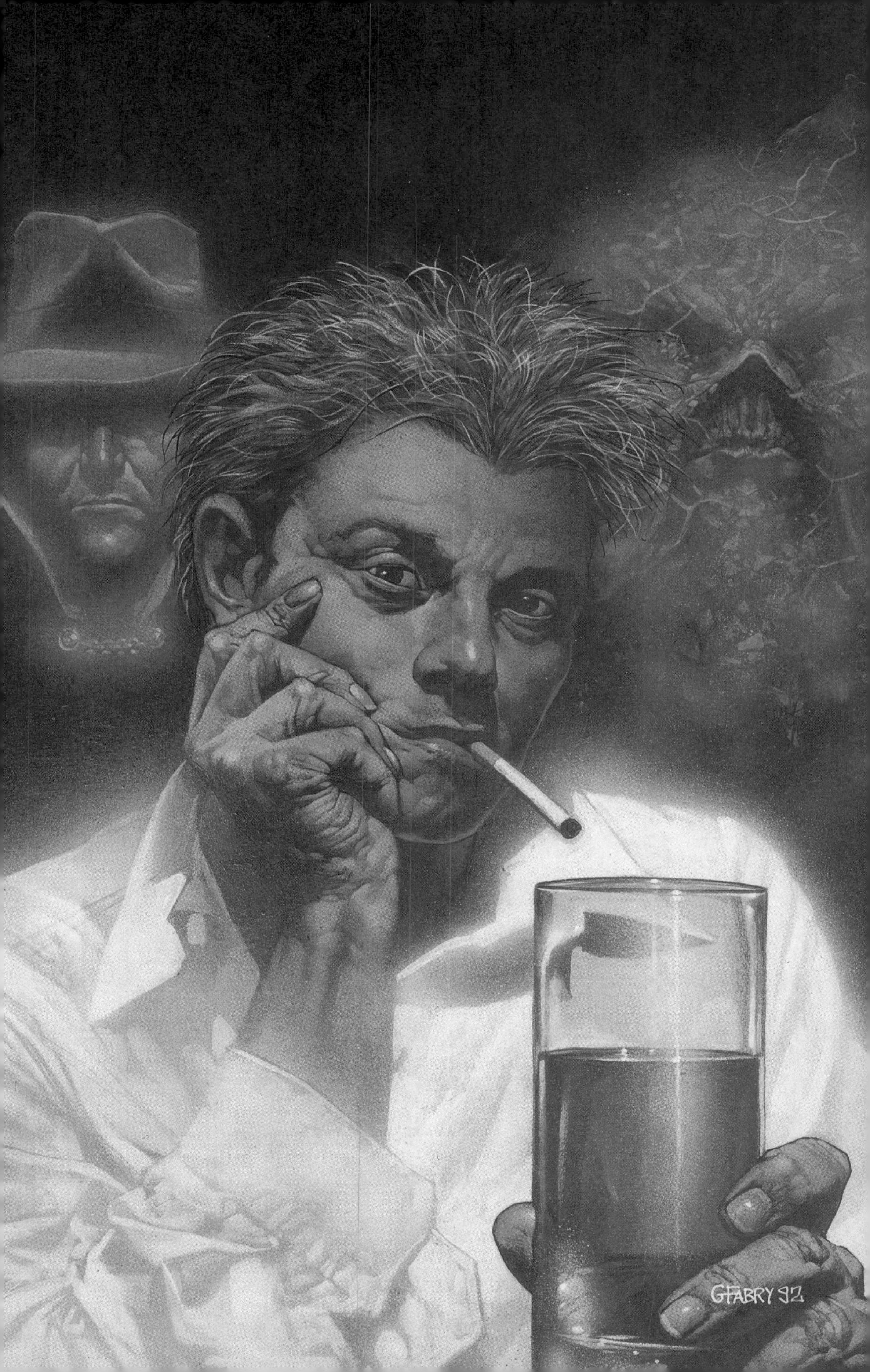
GFABRY 92

FORTY

GARTH ENNIS • writer
STEVE DILLON • artist
TOM ZIUKO • colors
gaspar • letters
STUART MOORE • editor

I HARDLY NOTICE WINTER TURNING INTO SPRING.

I'M DRIFTING THROUGH THE DAYS AND DOING NOTHING, IGNORING THE MAGICIAN'S NEED TO SCRABBLE IN THE DARK...

IT'S NOT THAT I'M *CONTENT*. BASTARDS RULE AND WANKERS WHINE AND BERKS BEND OVER, CHEEKS SPREAD WIDE...

SOD IT, I DUNNO.

SO THE MONTHS SHOOT BY AND *RIGHT NOW* GOES WITH 'EM, AND ALL I THINK ABOUT IS LOVE AND WAR TO COME...

AND THEN, THIS MORNING, I NOTICE THE DATE.

HERE, KIT? YOU KNOW WHAT DAY IT IS?

KIT?

John

DAILY Mirror

10 MAY 1993

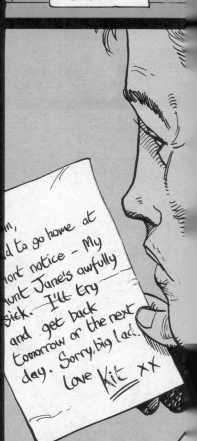

...n, ...d to go home at ...hort notice – My ...unt Jane's awfully ...sick. I'll try and get back tomorrow or the next day. Sorry, big lad. Love Kit xx

BOLLOCKS.

IS THIS THE CABBY'S ANSWER TO OSCAR WILDE?

PISS OFF, JOHN. WHAT'S THE SCORE?

WELL...I'VE JUST REMEMBERED SOMETHING. IT'S, uh...

IT'S ME BIRTH-DAY.

YOU'RE JOKIN'! HOW OLD ARE YOU?

FORTY.

FRIGGIN' HELL! JOHN CONSTANTINE THE FOGEY!

CAN I GIVE YOU ALL THE SHIT I GOT, THEN? "HEY, CHAS-D'YOU WANT YOUR ZIMMER?" "D'YOU NEED A HAND IN THE KHAZI, GRANDAD?"

CHRIST! WE ARE ON FORM...!

ANYWAY, LOOK: YOU COMIN' DOWN THE RED ROVER? KIT'S OUT OF TOWN, LIKE...

GOTTA KEEP IT IN YOUR TROUSERS, TONIGHT, EH?

SORRY, MATE, I CAN'T. I'M ON TILL SIX TOMORROW MORNING...

FRIGGIN' HURRY UP, CHANDLER!

AW, COME ON, CHAS! IT'S ME BIRTHDAY...!

I'M SORRY, LIKE, BUT WHAT CAN I DO? YOU KNOW WHAT THE MISSUS IS LIKE!

GIVE US A BELL TOMORROW, RIGHT? I'VE GOTTA GO.

BUGGER IT. SINCE WHEN DID I EVER HAVE A HAPPY BIRTHDAY, ANYWAY?

GIVE US TWO BOTTLES OF JACK DANIELS AND SIXTY SILK CUT, JANINE.

NOT YOUR USUAL, JOHN.

FORTY YEARS OF KNIVES IN THE BACK. THAT'S ALL I'VE MANAGED.

FORTY BLOODY YEARS...

S'POSE NOT.

ERE, YOU SHOULD'VE SEEN THE BLOKE IN BEFORE YOU! SIX FOOT SIX, BIG AS A BUS!

HE BOUGHT TEN CRATES OF TENNENTS SUPER, TEN BOTTLES OF BUSHMILLS AN' ALL THIS OTHER STUFF! I MEAN, I COULDN'T BELIEVE IT...

GLAD SOMEONE'S HAVING A GOOD TIME.

SEE YA!

HOW CAN I BE FORTY, FOR CRYING OUT LOUD?

AH, SHIT!

MY LIFE'S NOTHING TO CELEBRATE.

IS THAT WHY KIT'S IN BELFAST? WHY CHAS IS SNOWED UNDER? 'COS I'M MEANT TO HAVE A FRIGGING CRAP TIME OF IT?

GOT NO OTHER MATES. OH, I KNOW PEOPLE -- BUT THEY TWIG THERE'S SOMETHING NOT QUITE RIGHT AND KEEP THEIR DISTANCE.

THEY KNOW WHAT HAPPENS WHEN YOU GET TOO CLOSE.

WELL, HERE WE GO, GET DRUNK, GET MAUDLIN, SLIDE ON DOWN...

BLOODY HELL.

I'M FORTY, ALL RIGHT.

HEY, JOHNNY! CATCH!

JESUS--!

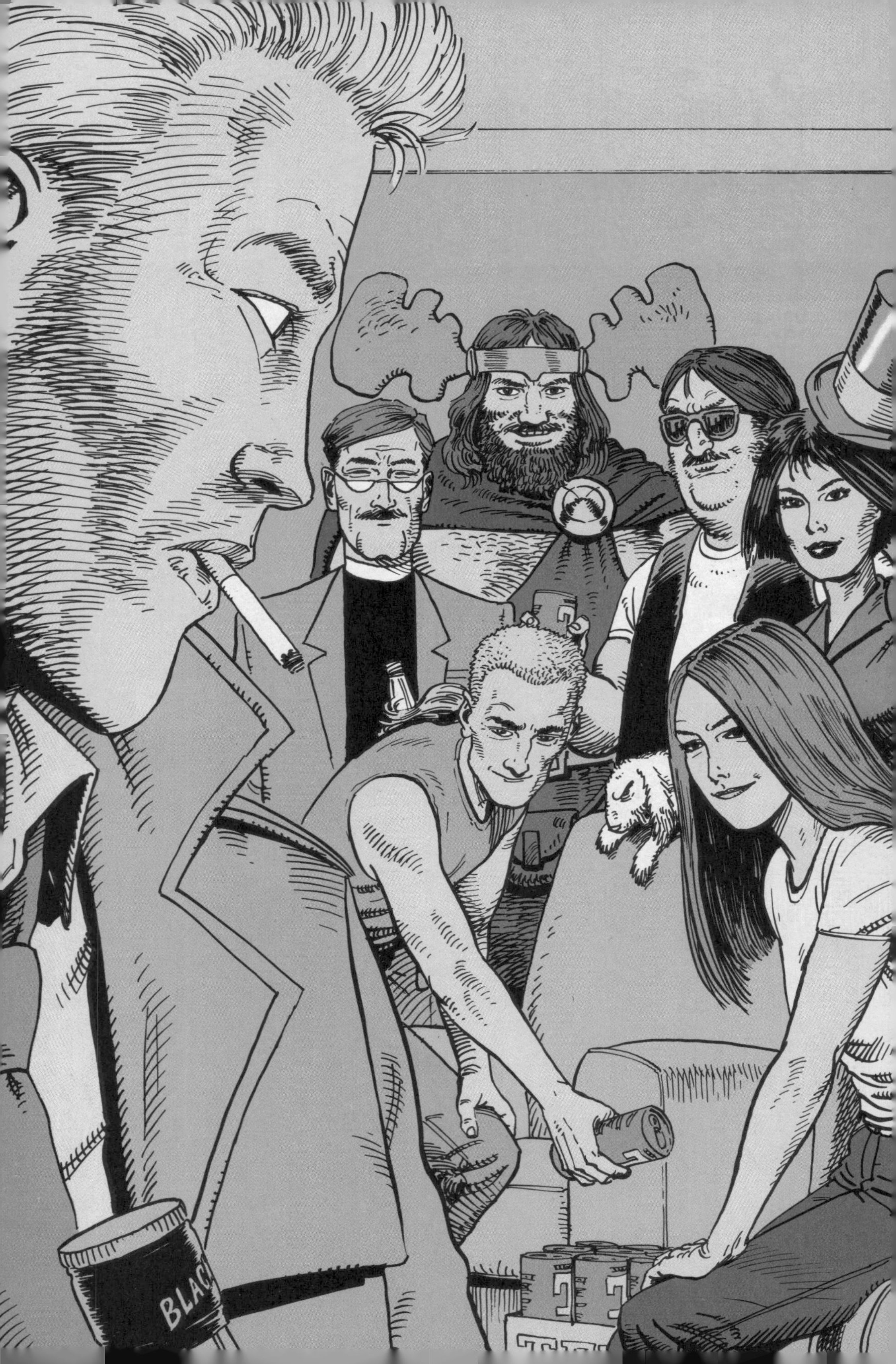

WHAT...

WHAT'S THIS?

IT'S YER *PARTY,* YE STUPID BASTARD...!

YOU'VE PLENTY OF FRIENDS, JOHNNY. JUST HAVE TO KNOW WHERE TO LOOK FOR THEM.

I DID.

COME ON, JOHN. YOU'VE A REPUTATION TO LIVE UP TO...

I HAVEN'T SEEN YOU SINCE LAST CHRISTMAS! AND YOU PUT *THIS* TOGETHER!

SCREW ME, THIS IS FRIGGIN' GREAT! I THOUGHT I WAS IN FOR ONE *MISERABLE* BLOODY NIGHT...

CAN'T BE DOWN ALL YOUR LIFE, JOHNNY.

er... I MEAN, EVEN *I* HAVE TO TAKE A BREAK FROM THE WAR ON CAPITALISM NOW AND THEN...

BLOODY HELL, IT'S NIGEL ENGELS...

NEVER THOUGHT I'D SEE *YOU* ON ME BIRTHDAY, SON.

WELL, YEAH. YOU GAVE ME QUITE A BIT TO THINK ABOUT, WITH THE ROYAL THING...

NOT JUST YOU, NIGE.

NOTICE HOW HE HAD SOME PUBLIC TROUBLE WITH THE MISSUS, JUST AFTER WE FINISHED? *POSSESSION* LEAVES YOU WITH *SCARS*... I HEAR HE GOT UP TO SOME WELL DODGY STUFF IN THE BEDROOM. AND... WELL...

I'M NOT GONNA DRAW YOU A PICTURE.

IS HE THE NIGEL ARCHER WANTED TAE DO THE *VOODOO* OAN THATCHER, AYE?

THAT'S HIM, HEADER.

BLOODY *IDIOT*...

I MEAN, DIDN'T HE KNOW WHO SHE HAD ON *HER* SIDE?

44

DON'T BE CRUEL, ELLIE. IT'S A *PARTY*, INNIT?

HOW'S LIFE WITH YOU, HEADER? AND RICK THE VIC...

I'M A'RIGHT, JOHNNY. I'M SURE THIS WEE NYAFF'S UP TAE NO FRIGGIN' GOOD, MIND YOU...

MAY THE LORD BLESS YOU AND KEEP YOU, HEADER.

ALL IS WELL WITH ME, JOHN, THANK YOU FOR ASKING.

I RECENTLY LOCATED THE BANNED LITERATURE YOU MENTIONED THE LAST TIME WE MET, IN THE ARCHBISHOP'S COLLECTION, THE USUAL PRICE...?

FOR A FORESKIN BIBLE? MAYBE.

WHAT'S UP, MANGE?

EFFIN' *IRONY*, HE SAID. PUTS ME MIND INTO THE EFFIN' RABBIT OFF ME STAGE ACT, LIKE.

IRONY.

YOU STILL DO THAT TRICK WHERE YOU PULL A MAGICIAN OUT OF A HAT?

GIMME A HAT AN I'LL EFFIN' SHOW YOU.

EFFIN' *SHITE.*

45

GONNA BE ONE OF THOSE NIGHTS...

SUITS ME.

THREE HOURS IN AND I'M PISSED AS A FART.

FRIG KNOWS HOW I GOT OUT HERE...

I...STUCK MY FINGER IN THE WOODPECKER'S HOLE...AN' THE WOODPECKER SAID...GOD BLESS MY SOUL...♪

TAKE IT OUT... TAKE IT OUT... RE-MOVE IT! ♪

WHAH--?

JOHN CONSTANTINE?

I HAD HOPED WE WOULD IGNORE THE COLD FACADE THAT OUR KIND DEEMS SO NECESSARY, IF ONLY AT THIS TIME OF CELEBRATION.

BUT I SEE THERE WILL BE NO HANDS CLASPED AGAINST THE DARK THIS NIGHT...

I SEE I MUST REMAIN A STRANGER.

OH CHRIST, THE POOR BASTARD...! ALL THOSE YEARS ON HIS OWN AND I...

I...

uh...

HUH-HUH... HUP!

HAHA HAHA HAHAHA!!

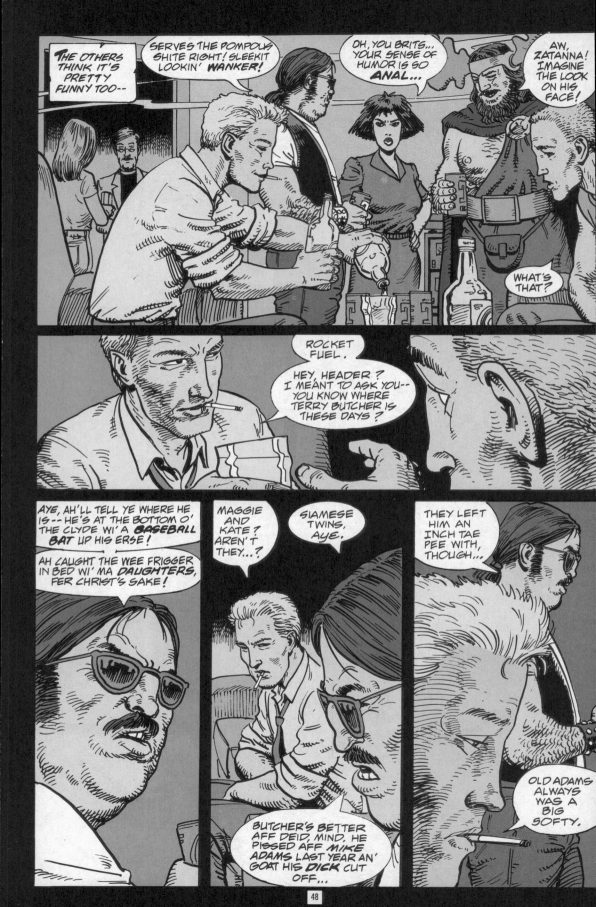

THE OTHERS THINK IT'S PRETTY FUNNY TOO--

SERVES THE POMPOUS SHITE RIGHT! SLEEKIT LOOKIN' *WANKER!*

OH, YOU BRITS... YOUR SENSE OF HUMOR IS SO *ANAL...*

AW, ZATANNA! IMAGINE THE LOOK ON HIS FACE!

WHAT'S THAT?

ROCKET FUEL.

HEY, HEADER? I MEANT TO ASK YOU-- YOU KNOW WHERE TERRY BUTCHER IS THESE DAYS?

AYE, AH'LL TELL YE WHERE HE IS -- HE'S AT THE BOTTOM O' THE CLYDE WI' A *BASEBALL BAT* UP HIS ERSE!

AH CAUGHT THE WEE FRIGGER IN BED WI' MA *DAUGHTERS,* FER CHRIST'S SAKE!

MAGGIE AND KATE? AREN'T THEY...?

SIAMESE TWINS, AYE.

THEY LEFT HIM AN INCH TAE PEE WITH, THOUGH...

BUTCHER'S BETTER AFF DEID, MIND. HE PISSED AFF *MIKE ADAMS* LAST YEAR AN' GOAT HIS *DICK* CUT OFF...

OLD ADAMS ALWAYS WAS A BIG SOFTY.

THE WITCHING HOUR...

TWO GRAND AND A JAR OF ANGEL SPUNK, FINAL OFFER.

EH? CONS'TINE! D'YOU SPIKE M'EFFIN BROC'LI?

BASSERDS... BASSERDS... ALL FRIGGIN' BASSERDS...!

WHAT...IS THE MEANING... OF THIS...?

MR. S. THING
THE SWAMP

YOU INVITED *HIM*? BLOODY HELL, MATE!

AW, COME ON. YOU TWO GO BACK *AGES*...

WELL, NOW YOU KNOW HOW I FEEL, TRYING TO TALK TO A BLOKE WHO SPEAKS AT SOD ALL MILES AN HOUR! GROW SOME EXTRA VOCAL CHORDS, YOU BERK!

AND IT'S ME *BIRTHDAY*.

INVITED... TO WHAT? I AM BECOMING... IMPATIENT...

I...DID NOT KNOW. I BEAR YOU NO... ILL WILL...AS SUCH--

OH, LUCKY OLD ME...

SHIT. I'M SORRY, LADS...

ALL RIGHT, ALL RIGHT! DON'T TAKE THE HUMP, SPROUT-BOLLOCKS!

I'VE GOT THIS FRIGGIN' MAGIC IDEA...

HEADER, TAKE NIGE HOME AND PICK UP HIS PLANT, WILL YOU?

WE'LL KEEP A RED FLAG FLYIN' HEEERE...

THEY'RE GONE TWENTY MINUTES. GOD KNOWS WHERE HEADER GOT HIS NEW HAT, BUT I'LL BET ONE LITTLE PIGGY'S OFF TO CASUALTY...

JEEZ, NIGEL! CHEECH AND CHONG, EAT YOUR HEART OUT!

NIGEL'S! HANDS OFF!

COUR

TAKE IT AWAY, MAESTRO...

OH, TREEBEARD! I KNEW YOU'D GROW UP ONE DAY!

OOHHHH...

"And they shall also make gardens... and eat the fruit of them..."

RIGHT! WHO'S GOAT THE RIZLAS?

CHEERS! YOU DRY IT OUT FOR US, YEAH?

YES.

I MUST GO NOW. MY FAMILY... NEEDS... MY PROTECTION...

RIGHT.

I'LL TRY AND LEAVE YOU ALONE FROM NOW ON, OKAY?

YOU ARE VERY DRUNK, CONSTANTINE.

GOODBYE.

THAT HIM AWAY, AYE?

YEAH.

AH'M TELLIN' YE, IF AH HAD ENOUGH PAPERS AH'D SKIN HIM UP AN' SMOKE HIM...

LOOK, FOR WHAT IT'S WORTH, RIGHT...

HERE WE GO... SHIT, IT'S BEEN BLEEDIN' AGES...!

I'M DEAD GOOD AT THIS, Y'KNOW. 'S THE CARDBOARD BIT AT THE END'S THE TRICKY BIT... APPARENTLY THEY DON'T DO THAT IN AMERICA...

NO. SO HOW DID YOU MEET JOHN, NIGEL?

WELL... OUR STUDENT UNION WAS HAUNTED, RIGHT? THIS SOCIOLOGY STUDENT JUMPED OUT A WINDOW ON ACID, AN' THEN HE CAME BACK...

SO CONSTANTINE SHOWED UP OUT OF NOWHERE AND SAID HE COULD GET RID OF IT. I THOUGHT HE WAS GOING TO DO AN EXORCISM...

HE JUST WALKED UP TO IT AND SAID "PISS OFF".

AND IT DID.

ALWAYS SEEM TO SCREW IT UP AT THE END.

THING WAS, HE SAID IT WAS THE CRAPPEST GHOST HE'D EVER SEEN...

I KEEP HEARING ABOUT THESE HUGE ONES YOU CAN DO, BUT IT SOUNDS A BIT OF A MYTH IF YOU ASK ME...

MONUMENTALLY STONED:

OH GOD...OH, I DON'T KNOW IF I CAN HANDLE THIS...

OH AYE ? WELL, AH'VE GOAT THE MUNCHIES SOMETHIN' SHOCKIN'...

M'I TUO FO YM ECAF...

YEAH...HE WON THIS POEM OF THE WEEK AWARD ONCE, RIGHT ? WENT APESHIT. "I MUST BE DOING WELL, 'COS THERE'S ONLY FIFTY-TWO OF THOSE"...

HEH. YOU SEEN THE STATE OF NIGEL ? MISTER MESSY...

HEY, WHAT'S THE SCOOP ON THIS KIT, JOHN ? LOOKS LIKE YOU'VE MET YOUR MATCH AT LAST...

BOLLOCKS...!

AW, COME ON. S'OVER A YEAR NOW. SHE MUST BE SOMETHING SPECIAL, eh?

SIX IN THE MORNING...

TAKE CARE, YOU LUNATIC. PLEASE.

LISSEN, I LOVE YOU. YOU'RE BEW'FUL...

YOU'RE PLAYING WITH FIRE, LITTLE BOY...

CHEERS, LADS. I'LL BE IN TOUCH.

EXCELLENT, JOHN. HEADER WILL NO DOUBT BE IN A FOUL MOOD WHEN ENGLAND ONCE AGAIN THRASH SCOTLAND IN THE CUP, BUT I ALWAYS LOOK FORWARD TO SEEING YOU...

AH, AWA' AN' THROW SHITE AT YERSELF!

SEE YOU, YOU SNEAKY SOD. WE GONNA SORT THIS FRIGGER SOON?

YOU BE CAREFUL ON THE WAY HOME NOW, NIGE...

YEAH, NO PROBS...! YOU'RE NOD SUDGA BAD BASSERD, Y' KNOW YAT? NOT SO BAAADD...

OH, YEAH...

ALL COPPERS ARE BASTARDS

55

THERE COMES A POINT AT ALL THE BEST PARTIES WHERE IT'S JUST TWO BLOKES AND A BOTTLE OF WHISKEY...

SO WHAT DO YOU SEE IN THE WHISKEY, JOHNNY?

I SEE... I SEE... I SEE ONE GODAWFUL FRIGGIN' HANGOVER AND HALF AN HOUR'S AGONY ON THE BOG IN THE MORNING...

IT IS THE MORNING.

mm.

TELL ME, THEN. HOW DOES IT FEEL TO BE FORTY?

I'M OFF TO A BLOODY WEIRD START, ANYWAY...

IT DOESN'T FEEL THAT DIFFERENT. JUST AN EASY WAY TO MARK OFF ANOTHER STAGE, KNOW WHAT I MEAN?

I'VE HAD ONE BUGGERED UP LIFE SO FAR, BUT BLOODY HELL--AT LEAST IT'S BEEN INTERESTING, LIKE.

CHEERS FOR THE PARTY, ANYWAY.

AH, I TOLD YOU I OWED YOU ONE.

IT'S GOOD FOR YOU, ANYWAY. YOU NEED TO LET YOUR GUARD DOWN NOW AND THEN, OR YOU'D FRIG YOURSELF UP ROYALLY.

56

I KNOW WHAT YOU MEAN ABOUT YOUR LIFE, JOHNNY. I KNOW YOU'VE MADE YOUR SHARE OF MISTAKES...

YOU'RE NOT PERFECT. YOU USUALLY END UP COVERED IN BLOOD WITH THE SHIT KICKED OUT OF YOU, PISSED OFF AT ALL THE BASTARDS WITH THE POWER THAT YOU JUST CAN'T TOUCH...

YOU'RE A RAKE AT THE GATES OF HELL.

THE POGUES WROTE A SONG THAT COULD'VE BEEN ABOUT YOU.

I MAY AS WELL TELL YOU, JOHNNY--YOU'RE IN FOR A BLOODY ROUGH COUPLE OF YEARS. YOU'VE PISSED OFF THE LAST PEOPLE YOU EVER SHOULD HAVE...

BUT I'LL BE THERE FOR YOU WHEN THE TIME COMES, SON.

BE LUCKY.

BLOODY CABBIES...

JOHN? YOU THERE, LOVE?

RABBIT SHITE...?

MY WEE FLAT... WHAT'VE THEY DONE TO MY WEE FLAT...?

WELL, WELL, WELL.

MUUUHHH...

M....M' FORDY, LUV... M' N' OLD MANNNN...

YOU SEEN THE STATE'VE THIS PLACE, WEE LAD?

YOU'RE A FRIGGIN' DEAD MAN.

The End

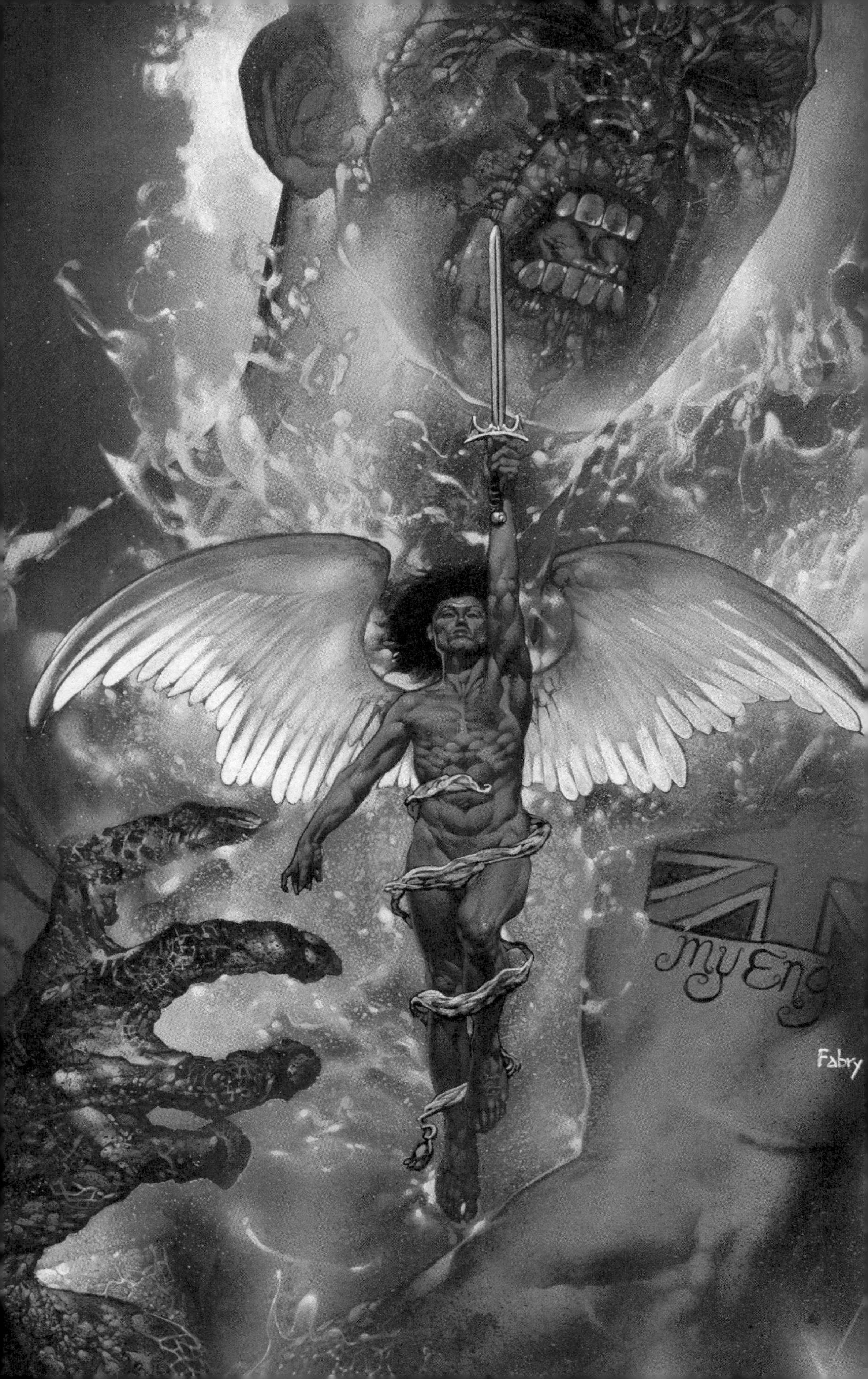
My Eng
Fabry

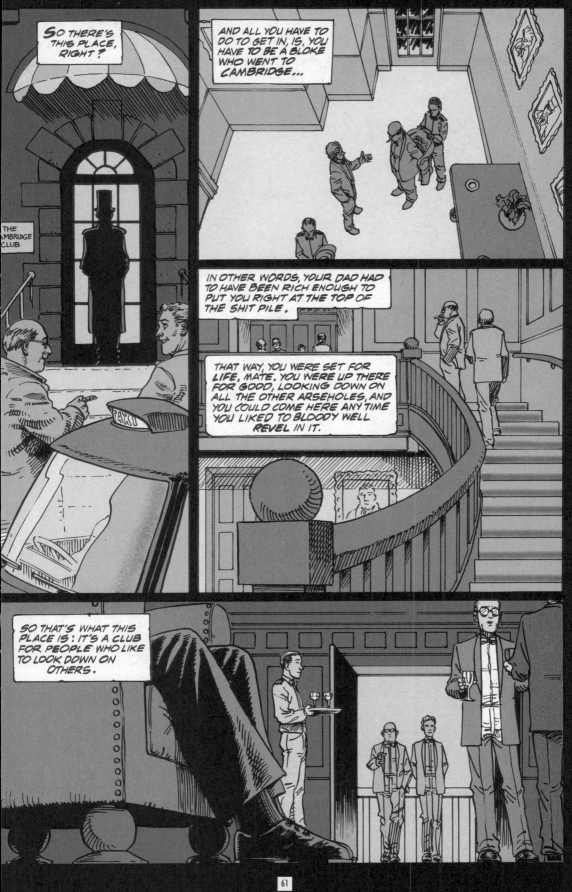

SO THERE'S THIS PLACE, RIGHT?

AND ALL YOU HAVE TO DO TO GET IN, IS, YOU HAVE TO BE A BLOKE WHO WENT TO CAMBRIDGE...

THE CAMBRIDGE CLUB

IN OTHER WORDS, YOUR DAD HAD TO HAVE BEEN RICH ENOUGH TO PUT YOU RIGHT AT THE TOP OF THE SHIT PILE.

THAT WAY, YOU WERE SET FOR LIFE, MATE. YOU WERE UP THERE FOR GOOD, LOOKING DOWN ON ALL THE OTHER ARSEHOLES, AND YOU COULD COME HERE ANY TIME YOU LIKED TO BLOODY WELL REVEL IN IT.

SO THAT'S WHAT THIS PLACE IS: IT'S A CLUB FOR PEOPLE WHO LIKE TO LOOK DOWN ON OTHERS.

FOR SNOBS.

FEAR and LOATHING PART ONE

FOR GOD and COUNTRY

GARTH ENNIS • writer
STEVE DILLON • artist
TOM ZIUKO • colors
gaspar • letters
STUART MOORE • editor

SOMETHING HAD BEEN WRONG FOR TWO YEARS NOW.

AND FRIGHTENED AS HE WAS TO ADMIT IT, WHAT WORRIED HIM WAS--

WELL, TO BEGIN AT THE BEGINNING...

HE WAS GABRIEL OF THE CHERUBIM, HE WAS DJIBRIL OF THE EL-KARRUBIYAN, THOSE BROUGHT NEAR TO ALLAH...

HE SOARED THROUGH THE FIRST SUNRISE AND SANG HIS JOY TO THE FIRST BORN OF THE WORLD, AND EVERY LIVING THING LEARNT HOW TO SMILE.

HE'D WALKED THROUGH BABYLON WITH ROSES IN HIS HAIR. HE'D GIVEN THE SUMERIANS WATER OF LIFE. HE'D COVERED STIRRING SLEEPERS WITH HIS WINGS BENEATH THE PYRAMIDS...

IT WAS THE WILL OF THE LORD.

AND...

63

HE'D BATHED IN ASSYRIAN BLOOD, SPIKED EGYPTIAN INFANTS HIGH ON SPEARS, TORN EYES AND GUTS AND RIBS AND JAWS FROM BODIES OF STILL LIVING MEN--

SODOM AND GOMORRAH DIED IN AN APOCALYPSE OF FIRE, THOUGH WHY ONE MAN SHOULD NOT HAVE ANOTHER, HE DIDN'T KNOW, JUST DID AS HE WAS BID--

THE WILL OF THE LORD.

HE'D COMMITTED RAPE BEHIND A CARPENTER'S IN NAZARETH, AND A CYCLE OF AGONY BEGAN THAT ENDED ON A HILL ABOVE JERUSALEM...

THE WILL OF THE LORD.

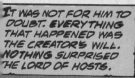
IT WAS NOT FOR HIM TO DOUBT. EVERYTHING THAT HAPPENED WAS THE CREATOR'S WILL. NOTHING SURPRISED THE LORD OF HOSTS.

SO...

SO CONSTANTINE WAS RIGHT. THE MAN HE'D SPOKEN TO--CHARLES PATTERSON--WAS A BULLY AND A RACIST THUG. A SINNER.

SO WHY HAD HE, GABRIEL, EVEN BEEN ALLOWED TO TALK TO HIM? WHY HADN'T HE AT LEAST BEEN REPRIMANDED?

THE WILL OF THE LORD?

AND WHAT WAS WILLED FOR HIM NOW, THEN? WHY WAS HE SUDDENLY HEADED IN THIS STRANGEST OF DIRECTIONS?

HIS HEART FULL OF TROUBLES, THE ARCHANGEL DECIDED TO TAKE THE AIR.

HE WHAT?

HE *LEFT*, SIR... USUALLY HE'S THERE BY THE FIRE ONE MINUTE AND DIS-APPEARED THE NEXT, BUT TONIGHT HE *WALKED* OUT.

GOD, THIS IS *UNBELIEVABLE--!* I MEAN, DAMN! DAMN AND *BUGGER!*

LOOK, YOU'LL HAVE TO FOLLOW HIM, D'YOU UNDERSTAND?

BUT I'M ON DUTY, SIR!

FRIG YOUR DUTY. YOU FOLLOW HIM AND REPORT TO ME OR I'LL HAVE YOUR BALLS ON A STICK, YOU LITTLE TURD.

=KLIK=

STAFF ONLY

I SAY, THOMPSON--THREE MORE PINK GINS AND A COGNAC! BE QUICK ABOUT IT, AND YOU SHALL HAVE A SHILLING!

A SHILLING! SPLENDID, OINKERS!

STICK IT UP YOUR ARSE, YOU OLD QUEER.

I SEE YOU STILL KNOW THE WAY TO A GIRL'S HEART...

VIA HER KNICKERS?

YOU DIRTY OUL' BUGGER!

AW, LESS OF THE OLD! THINK I WANNA BE REMINDED?

AH, YOU'RE DOIN' RIGHTLY. WHEN MY DA REACHED FORTY HE WAS HALF DEAD'VE DRINK, SO HE WAS...

AWAY OUTTA THAT. YOU THINK YOU CAN WRECK MY FLAT AN' CHARM YOUR WAY OUT'VE IT WITH A QUICK SEEIN' TO? YOUR ARSE, MATE!

HMMM...D'YOU FANCY A CUP'VE TEA?

YEAH.

THERE'S THAT BLOODY "F" WORD AGAIN.

SO D'YOU FORGIVE ME FOR THE PARTY, THEN?

GOOD. MAKE US ONE WHILE YOU'RE AT IT, WILL YOU?

I'M GOING OUT TONIGHT, LUV. FORGOT TO TELL YOU.

AYE, YOU'RE FINE. I'VE TO FINISH THAT COVER FOR THE NEW AMIS BOOK, ANYWAY.

IS THIS ANOTHER EXPLORATION OF THE COMPLEXITIES OF HIS OWN ARSEHOLE?

AW JOHN, WHO CARES?

IT'S JUST A HACK JOB. I'LL STRING A COUPLA BITS'VE LACE OVER A FEW LEAVES AND PAINT THE BACKGROUND TO LOOK LIKE STONE. BALLACKHEAD IN THE OFFICE'LL STICK A WEE BORDER ROUND IT AN' CALL IT POST MODERN, AN' AWAY YOU GO.

YOUR HAIR'S NICE LIKE THAT...

Y'KNOW, I'M ALWAYS MEANING TO TELL YOU YOURS IS NICE.

AWWWW...

AND THAT YOU'RE EVERYTHING TO ME, KIT.

HE REMEMBERED THE LOOK UPON THE FACE OF ABRAHAM: "YES, LORD. I WILL TAKE MY SON ISAAC AND MAKE OF HIM A BURNT OFFERING TO THEE..."

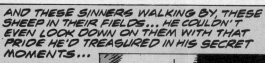

ACCEPTANCE. FAITH. TRUE FAITH.

HOW HE LONGED TO REGAIN IT.

AND THESE SINNERS WALKING BY, THESE SHEEP IN THEIR FIELDS... HE COULDN'T EVEN LOOK DOWN ON THEM WITH THAT PRIDE HE'D TREASURED IN HIS SECRET MOMENTS...

THE DOUBT HAD KILLED IT STONE DEAD.

THE DOUBT THAT CONSTANTINE HAD BEGUN, OH LORD, WHAT WAS IT DOING TO HIM?

WHAT?

OH!

I'M SO SORRY, I DIDN'T SEE YOU! I'M SO STUPID SOME-TIMES...

WELL *DON'T* SAY ANYTHING, THEN! ROTTEN *SNOB!*

THAT--

THAT'S WHAT *CONSTANTINE* CALLS HIM--AND THAT *DEMON WITCH,* AND THE WHOLE PACK OF *JACKALS--*

WAIT!

PLEASE, I-I DID NOT MEAN TO--

I--

I AM SORRY.

70

WELL, THAT'S...

THAT'S OKAY...

I, ah, I SHOULD NOT HAVE BEEN SO HAUGHTY. I WAS DIS-TRACTED...

I CAN ONLY BEG FOR-GIVENESS.

OH, YOU DON'T HAVE TO SAY THAT... LOOK, ARE YOU ALL RIGHT?

I MEAN, D'YOU WANT TO TALK, OR SOMETHING? BECAUSE YOU' SEEM AWFULLY WOUND UP...

I... I BELIEVE I WOULD LIKE THAT...

OKAY.

I'M JULIE, BY THE WAY.

GABRIEL.

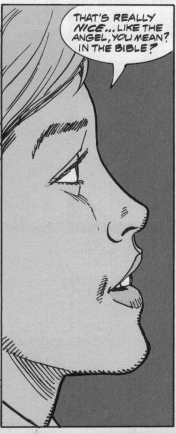

THAT'S REALLY NICE... LIKE THE ANGEL, YOU MEAN? IN THE BIBLE?

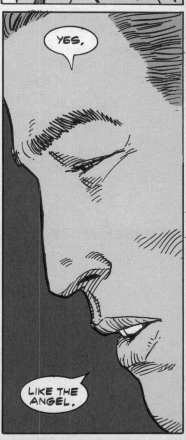

YES,

LIKE THE ANGEL.

POCKET SIZED AND EVERYTHING. CHEERS, RICK.

MY PLEASURE.

AH, JOY. NECTAR OF THE GODS...

IF YOU SAY SO. WHAT YOU GOT IN MIND FOR IT, ANYWAY?

NOW JOHN... I HAVE NO MORE INTENTION OF REVEALING MY PLANS FOR THIS THAN YOU HAVE YOURS FOR THAT FINE VOLUME BEFORE YOU...

HMMM?

AH, JOHN. YOU'LL BE IN HEAVEN HALF AN HOUR BEFORE THE DEVIL KNOWS YOU'RE DEAD.

I SHALL BE OFF, THEN...

HEY, JOHN! JOHNNY!

BLOODY HELL! DEZ! WHERE'VE YOU BEEN HIDING?

HIDING BOLLOCKS, SON! SEE WHO'S DOWN FROM BRUM?

'LO.

GEORGE...? YOU'VE CHANGED, MATE!

I'LL GET 'EM IN, UH...

REVEREND NEILSEN. RICK. A SMALL SHERRY WOULD BE NICE.

'S'ME FIRST TIME BACK IN THE SMOKE SINCE '89, JOHN!

LEAST YOU'VE STILL GOT THE ACCENT. FRIG ME... LAST TIME I SAW YOU, YOU WERE WHAT? EIGHTEEN?

YEAH. I CAN DO BRUMMIE, IF YOU WANT.

"Y'ARRIGHT, LOYKE? BEERMING 'AM, THAT'S ME, LOYKE, ME NAME'S BAARRY. SO'S ME MATE'S. AND'IS."

NOT BAD. WHY'D YOU LEAVE BRUM, THEN?

IMMENSE GOOD TASTE, I SHOULD IMAGINE...

'COS SOME BASTARD BURNT ME HOUSE DOWN, THAT'S WHY.

ME AN' THESE TWO LADS FROM WREXHAM WERE SQUATTIN', RIGHT? SO ONE NIGHT I COME HOME AND THERE'S THIS DICKHEAD *ON FIRE* IN THE FRIGGIN' GARDEN...

"I COULDN'T BLOODY *BELIEVE* IT! I WAS TRYIN' TO WORK OUT HOW THE FRIG TO *PUT HIM OUT*..."

"AN' THEN I SAW WHAT HE'D BEEN UP TO."

DID YOU HELP HIM?

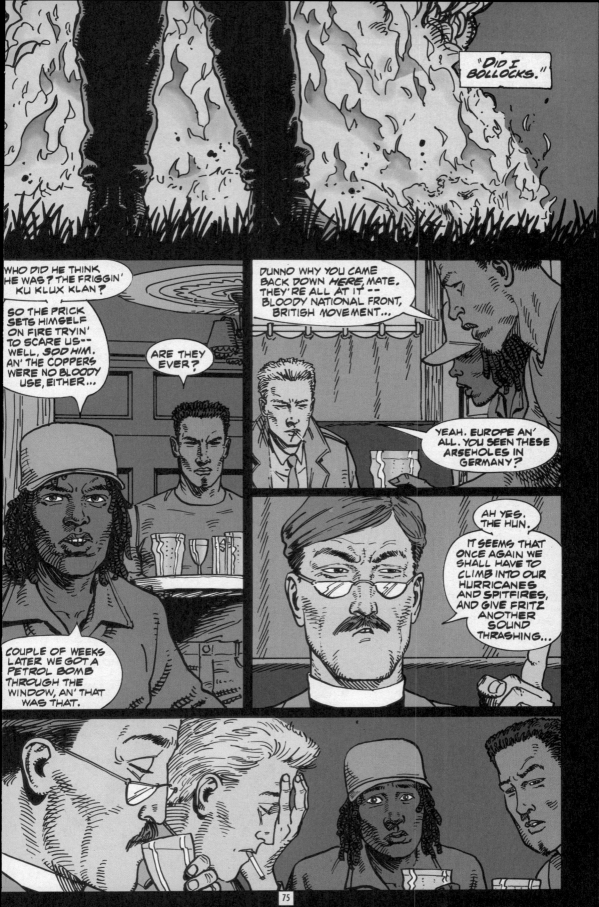

"DID I BOLLOCKS."

WHO DID HE THINK HE WAS? THE FRIGGIN' KU KLUX KLAN?

SO THE PRICK SETS HIMSELF ON FIRE TRYIN' TO SCARE US-- WELL, SOD HIM. AN' THE COPPERS WERE NO BLOODY USE, EITHER...

ARE THEY EVER?

DUNNO WHY YOU CAME BACK DOWN HERE, MATE. THEY'RE ALL AT IT -- BLOODY NATIONAL FRONT, BRITISH MOVEMENT...

YEAH. EUROPE AN' ALL. YOU SEEN THESE ARSEHOLES IN GERMANY?

COUPLE OF WEEKS LATER WE GOT A PETROL BOMB THROUGH THE WINDOW, AN' THAT WAS THAT.

AH YES. THE HUN.

IT SEEMS THAT ONCE AGAIN WE SHALL HAVE TO CLIMB INTO OUR HURRICANES AND SPITFIRES, AND GIVE FRITZ ANOTHER SOUND THRASHING...

75

YEAH, WELL... I MEAN, THEY'RE ALL GOING TO HAVE TO WATCH THEIR ARSES IF THEY KEEP TRYIN' THIS SHIT ON US, RIGHT?

YOU SEE THAT THING IN LOS ANGELES LAST YEAR? THAT'S THE CLEAREST BLOODY WARNING THEY'RE GONNA GET, BUT THEY'RE TOO STUPID TO FACE IT...

OI! CONSTANTINE! PHONE FOR YOU!

RIGHT...

YEAH? RIGHT.

TOLD YOU, DIDN'T I?

WE'RE IN BUSINESS, THEN. TAKE IT SLOWLY, RIGHT?

RING US BACK HERE TOMORROW, ABOUT NOON.

GOOD NEWS, JOHN?

YEAH.

FANCY A LITTLE CELEBRATION?

AW, GREAT! JANINE SAYS IT'S DRINKS ON THE HOUSE, LADS!

ARE YOU SURE YOU WOULDN'T LIKE SOMETHING?

NO THANK YOU. I DON'T DRINK.

YOU'RE ONE OF A DYING BREED THESE DAYS, GABRIEL.

SO WHAT'S UP?

I AM AN ANGEL OF THE LORD OUR GOD, AND FOR THE FIRST TIME IN MY EXISTENCE I AM UNCERTAIN OF MY FUTURE. OF EVERYTHING.

I AM SCARED.

I....

IT'S MY FATHER.

MY FATHER IS A MAN OF EXTREMES. MORAL DISTINCTIONS ARE, FOR HIM, A SIMPLE QUESTION OF RIGHT AND WRONG.

OF BLACK AND WHITE.

MY BROTHERS AND I ARE THERE-FORE... WE STRIVE TO BE ABOVE REPROACH.

I MYSELF HAVE... ASSISTED IN DISCIPLINING SOME OF THE YOUNGER BOYS.

BUT MY ELDEST BROTHER, THE MOST PROMISING OF US ALL, HE... HE WAS WORSE THAN ANY OF THEM. MY FATHER WAS STERNEST OF ALL WITH HIM.

WHAT HAPPENED TO HIM?

HE FELL.

78

SO ARE YOU IN TROUBLE TOO? WITH YOUR FATHER?

I DON'T KNOW.

I MAY BE.

I APOLOGIZE. THIS MUST ALL SEEM MEANINGLESS TO YOU.

NO! OH NO. NOT AT ALL.

ANYWAY, YOU'VE GOT SUCH A LOVELY VOICE I COULD LISTEN TO YOU ALL NIGHT.

WELL, WHY DO YOU THINK YOU'RE...

A MAN SAID SOMETHING TO ME.

A MAN NAMED CONSTANTINE.

79

I CAN HEAR THE OLD DAYS CALLING...

SOME OF THE SHIT I GOT OFF WITH LAST YEAR, IT'S LIKE '83 ALL OVER AGAIN. OUT OF THE SHADOWS AND "ALL RIGHT, SQUIRE? TRUST ME." AND GONE BEFORE YOU KNOW IT.

CHRIST, THAT WAS A LAUGH...

SO I REMIND MYSELF IT WASN'T, IT WAS DEAD MATES AND LOST SOULS AND COLD NIGHTS WITH THE BOTTLE WHILE THE GHOSTS HOWLED ROUND THE DOOR...

AND NOW IT'S DIFFERENT ANYWAY.

KIT...

AND SAYING HER NAME MAKES ME MORE DETERMINED.

AND I ALMOST BELIEVE MY OWN BULLSHIT.

HE TOLD HER MORE TONIGHT THAN HE HIMSELF HAD EVER DARED THINK BEFORE.

"MAYBE YOU WORRY TOO MUCH" SHE SAID. "JUST BECAUSE THIS CONSTANTINE MAKES NASTY REMARKS DOESN'T MEAN YOUR DAD'S ANGRY WITH YOU."

"HE SOUNDS LIKE A RAT, ANYWAY, THIS GUY. FORGET HIM."

EVERY TIME SHE SMILED THERE WAS A LITTLE LAUGH DANCING ON HER LIPS...

YOU LONELY, LUV?

AND SHE'D BE THERE AGAIN TOMORROW, IF HE WANTED TO TALK SOME MORE.

M-MR. PATTERSON?

mmf?

THE BEGINNERS NIETZSCHE

WHAT'RE *YOU* DOING HERE? I'VE BEEN SITTING HERE ALL NIGHT WAITING FOR YOU TO CALL!

I DIDN'T WANNA PHONE. I'M SCARED, MR. PATTERSON. I'M *SHITTING BRICKS!*

WHAT D'YOU MEAN? *WHAT HAPPENED?*

HE ENDED UP TALKING TO SOME DO-GOODER BIRD, THAT'S WHAT!

I MEAN, HE NEAR AS DAMN IT TOLD HER WHO HE WAS!

HE'S *SPOOKED*, MR. PATTERSON, AND I'LL TELL YOU WHO'S BLOODY WELL DOING IT: *CONSTANTINE.*

I WANT OUT OF THIS, ALL RIGHT? IT'S GETTING WELL OUT OF ORDER-- D'YOU EVEN REMEMBER WHAT HE *IS*, FOR GOD'S SAKE?

AND IF THAT CREEPY SOD'S STICKING HIS NOSE IN, THAT'S IT. I *QUIT!*

NO

YOU

FRIGGING

DON'T

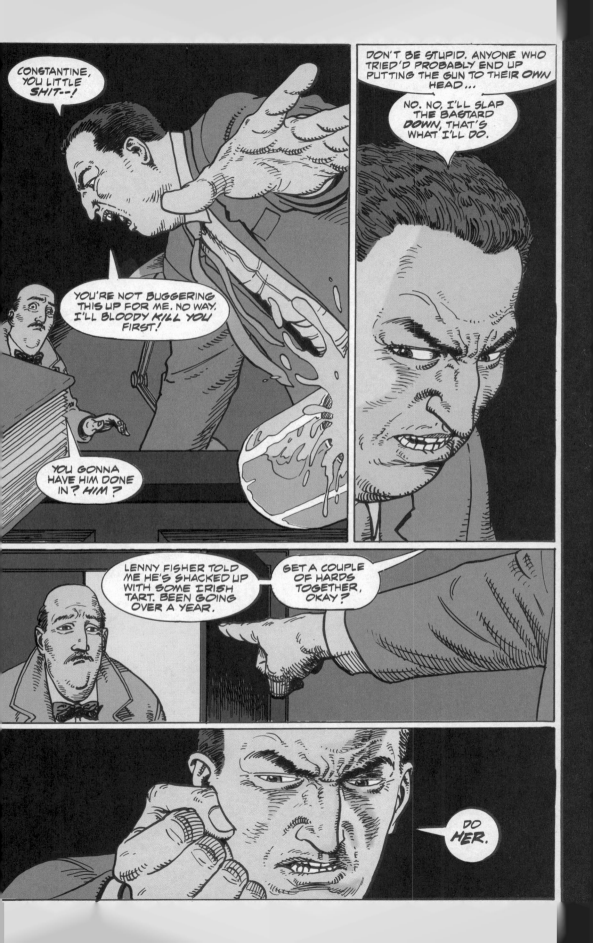

CONSTANTINE, YOU LITTLE SHIT--!

DON'T BE STUPID. ANYONE WHO TRIED'D PROBABLY END UP PUTTING THE GUN TO THEIR OWN HEAD...

NO. NO, I'LL SLAP THE BASTARD DOWN, THAT'S WHAT I'LL DO.

YOU'RE NOT BUGGERING THIS UP FOR ME. NO WAY, I'LL BLOODY KILL YOU FIRST!

YOU GONNA HAVE HIM DONE IN? HIM?

LENNY FISHER TOLD ME HE'S SHACKED UP WITH SOME IRISH TART. BEEN GOING OVER A YEAR.

GET A COUPLE OF HARDS TOGETHER, OKAY?

DO HER.

Y-YES, MR. PATTERSON.

NEXT: HEADING FOR A FALL

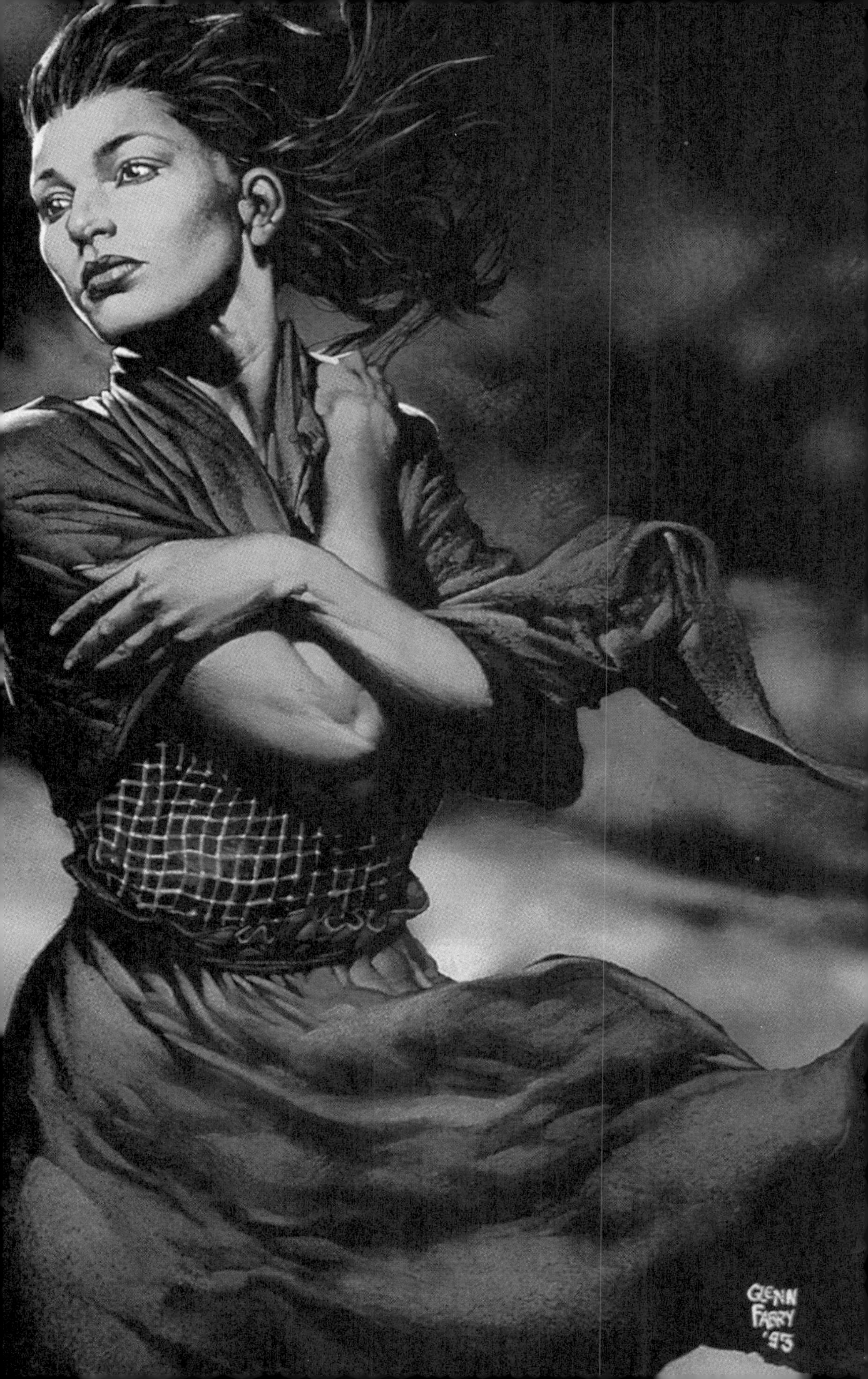
GLENN
FABRY
'95

YOU'RE AWFULLY HUNG UP ABOUT ALL THIS, GABRIEL. YOU DON'T EVEN SEEM TO KNOW WHAT IT IS YOU'VE DONE WRONG, BUT YOU'RE TERRIFIED OF YOUR FATHER ANYWAY...

HE MUST BE REALLY *STRICT.*

HE IS.

OH, GABRIEL...

YOU'RE A GROWN MAN, YOU KNOW. IT CAN'T BE GOOD FOR YOU TO LIVE IN HIS SHADOW LIKE THIS... MAYBE IT'S TIME YOU *MOVED OUT* ON YOUR OWN.

THAT ISN'T POSSIBLE.

LOOK AT YOU.

WHAT DID HE DO TO MAKE YOU FEEL SO *SCARED* AND *GUILTY?* IT SHOULDN'T BE LIKE THAT...

NO GUILT, *eh,* GABRIEL?

NO GUILT.

GARTH ENNIS • writer
STEVE DILLON • artist
TOM ZIUKO • colors
gaspar • letters
STUART MOORE • editor

FEAR and LOATHING PART TWO
LONDON KILLS ME

I DUNNO, CLAIRE. I'M STILL THINKIN' ABOUT IT, Y'KNOW?

AYE, I KNOW I'M ALWAYS MOANIN' ABOUT LONDON, BUT--YEAH, WELL, THERE *IS* JOHN. NO, I DON'T THINK HE'D WANT TO MOVE.

AH, YOU DIRTY WEE BITCH! HE'S NOT YOUR TYPE, ANY--WAY...!

YOUR TYPE? BUCK EEJITS WITH A LOT'VE SPARE CASH, WASN'T IT?

CLAIRE, YOUR PATRICK WAS SO BLOODY STUPID HE TRIED TO GO JOYRIDIN' IN A STEAMROLLER--

OH, DON'T TRY AN'-- OH, DON'T EVEN TALK TO ME!

AYE, ALL RIGHT.

I'LL HAVE TO AWAY ON TOO. I THINK I HEAR YER MAN ON THE STAIRS, THERE...

WHAT? SEE WHEN I GET YOU, WEE GIRL, I'M GONNA WASH YOUR MOUTH OUT WITH SOAP!

AYE. AYE, RIGHT.

SEE YA.

JOHN...?

JESUS--!

WHAT...

WHAT...

FRIG ME, SHE'S GORGEOUS...

CRYIN' SHAME, INNIT?

RIGHT.

GET OUT'VE HERE. NOW. RIGHT FRIGGIN' NOW...

I MEAN IT...

BE EASIER IF YOU DON'T GIVE US ANY TROUBLE, LUV. YOU'VE GOT THE WRONG BOYFRIEND, THAT'S ALL THERE IS TO IT...

GRAB HOLD'VE HER, WILL YOU, SAM?

YOU'LL BE SORT OF A WARNING, KNOW WHAT I MEAN?

LAST CHANCE, SON.

I THINK I'VE SHAT MESELF! HAHAHAHA!

HAHAHAHAHA! YOU HEAR THIS, MICKEY? IT'S ME LAST CHANCE!

AH--!

AAOW!

ME FACE! SHE'S RIPPED ME FRIGGIN' FACE OFF--!

GET HER, SAM!

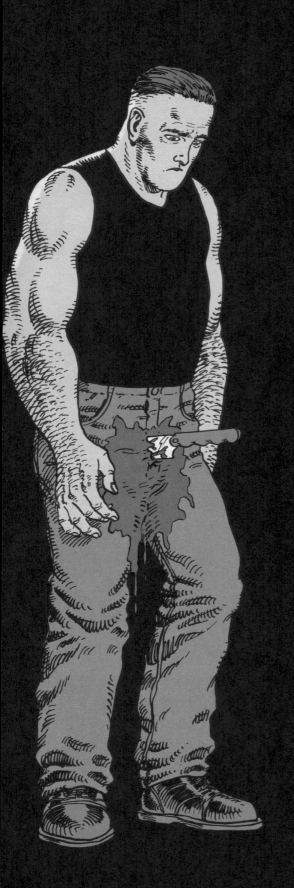

M-M-MICKY?

MIIICKYYY!!

GOOD GOD...!

YES...YES... SLOW *DOWN*, WILL YOU?

NO, FORGET HER.

HHHH....

WHAT'S UP?

APPARENTLY THE BITCH HAS TEETH...

I THINK-- WELL, LIKE IT OR NOT, WE'RE GOING TO HAVE TO TAKE CONSTANTINE DIRECTLY.

GET A CAR READY, AND THE APPROPRIATE NEANDERTHALS, I'M COMING TOO.

FINE.

RIGHT...YOU OKAY, MR. PATTERSON?

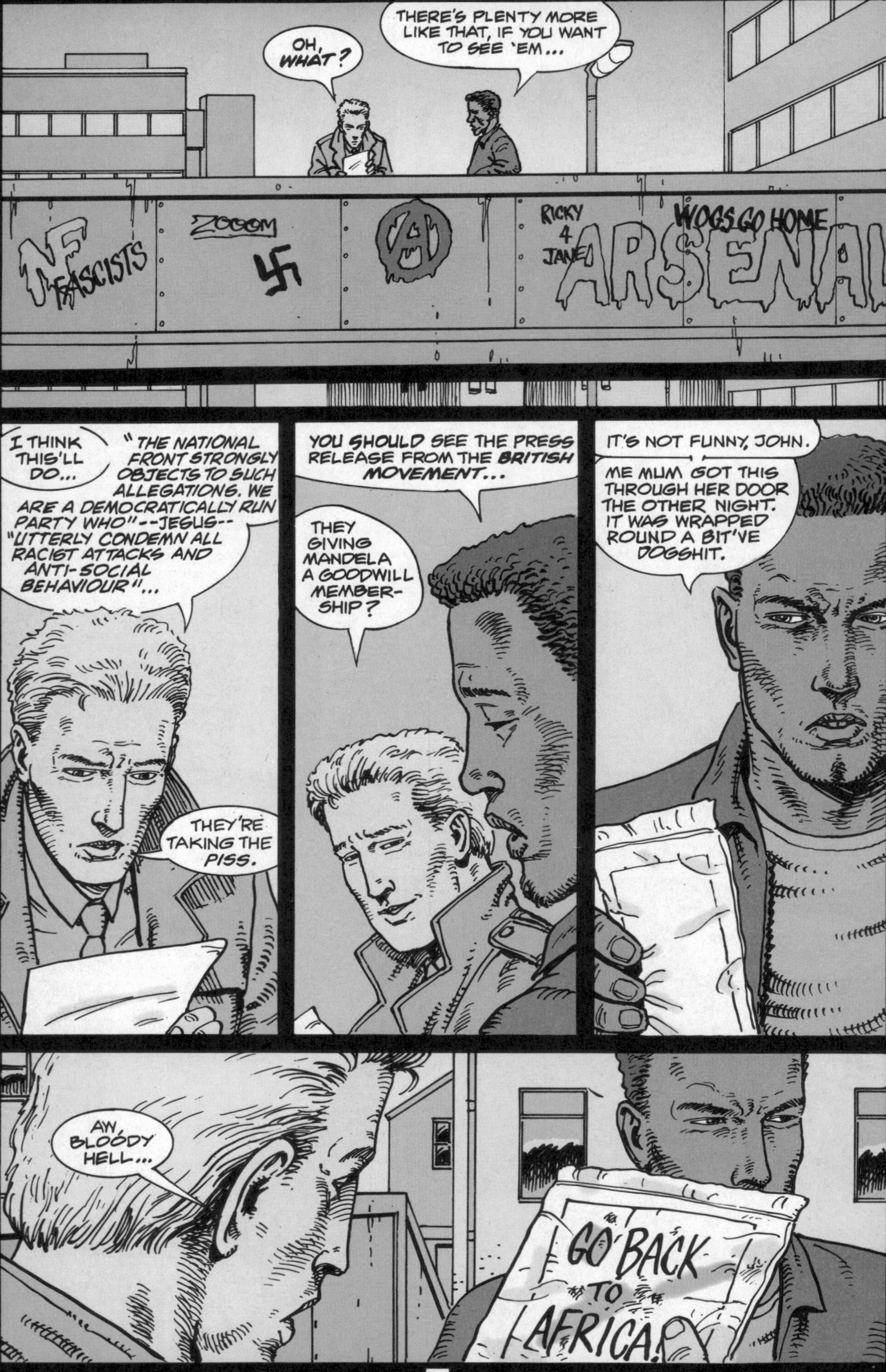

OH, WHAT?
THERE'S PLENTY MORE LIKE THAT, IF YOU WANT TO SEE 'EM...
NF
FASCISTS
ZOOOM
RICKY 4 JANE
WOGS GO HOME
ARSENAL
I THINK THIS'LL DO...
"THE NATIONAL FRONT STRONGLY OBJECTS TO SUCH ALLEGATIONS. WE ARE A DEMOCRATICALLY RUN PARTY WHO"--JESUS--"UTTERLY CONDEMN ALL RACIST ATTACKS AND ANTI-SOCIAL BEHAVIOUR"...
THEY'RE TAKING THE PISS.
YOU SHOULD SEE THE PRESS RELEASE FROM THE BRITISH MOVEMENT...
THEY GIVING MANDELA A GOODWILL MEMBER-SHIP?
IT'S NOT FUNNY, JOHN.
ME MUM GOT THIS THROUGH HER DOOR THE OTHER NIGHT. IT WAS WRAPPED ROUND A BIT'VE DOGSHIT.
AW, BLOODY HELL...
GO BACK TO AFRICA!

I'M SORRY, DEZ. YOU'RE GONNA GET A LOT MORE'VE IT, TOO.

YEAH, YOUNG GEORGE IS WOUND UP TO NINETY, READY TO DO SOMEONE SOME DAMAGE...

SIGN'VE THE TIMES, INNIT? ALL THESE LITTLE FRIGGERS OUT OF WORK, LOOKING FOR THE ENEMY WITHIN.

IT'S NOT LIKE I TOOK THEIR BLOODY JOBS...

END OF THE CENTURY, TOO. ALL THE ARSE-HOLES COME CRAWLING OUT OF THE WOODWORK.

TELL YOU WHAT-- THERE'S THIS LITTLE NAZI TOSSER I KNOW CALLED CHARLIE PATTERSON. I'M BUSY NOW, BUT I COULD HAVE A BIT OF A SNIFF IF YOU WANT...

CHEERS-- JESUS!

95

FRIGGIN' HELL! GET OFF HIM!

PISS OFF CHOCOLATE--

BRING THE NIGGER TOO! COME ON!

RUUHH!

AWH--!

OFF!

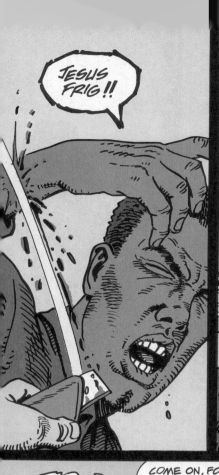

JESUS FRIG !!

AAAAHH!

AWH--!

COME ON, FOR GOD'S SAKE! GET HIM IN THE CAR!

COME ON!

...WELL, LOOK, CHAS: IF YOU SEE HIM, TELL HIM NOT TO GO HOME. TELL HIM I'M IN THE *GREEN MAN* UP NEAR MUSWELL HILL AND I WANT TO SEE HIM *NOW*, RIGHT?

AYE, I KNOW IT'S A LONG WAY--NO, I'M NOT IN TROUBLE--

CHAS, WOULD YOU JUST *DO* IT FOR US, *PLEASE*?

AW, I'M SORRY. OKAY. AYE.

'BYE.

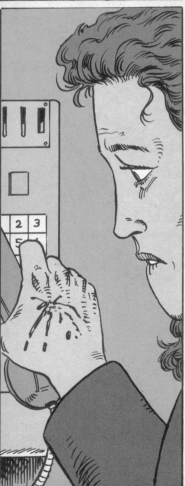

SHE'D BEEN DOING PRETTY WELL, SHE THOUGHT. KNOCK THE BADDIES' SHITE IN, GET TO SOMEWHERE SAFE, SWITCH ON THE OUL' ICE WOMAN BIT AND GET READY TO GIVE CONSTANTINE THE BALLACKIN' OF HIS *LIFE*--

AYE, WELL. NOBODY'S PERFECT.

LAD

WAKE HIM UP.

AAAH--!

I THOUGHT IT WAS MEANT TO BE IMPOSSIBLE TO SNEAK UP ON YOU, CONSTANTINE.

LOSING YOUR TOUCH.

YEAH. ME DICKLESS LITTLE SHIT DETECTOR MUST BE ON THE BLINK.

NICE ONE, SCHWARZENEGGER. BEEN GIVING IT A BIT EXTRA ON THE FIVE-KNUCKLE SHUFFLE, HAVE WE?

SHOW HIM HIS FRIEND.

YOU SHOULD'VE STAYED AWAY FROM THE ARCHANGEL, YOU KNOW. NOW...

WELL, WHAT CAN I SAY?

DEZ?

TAKE THE BAG OFF.

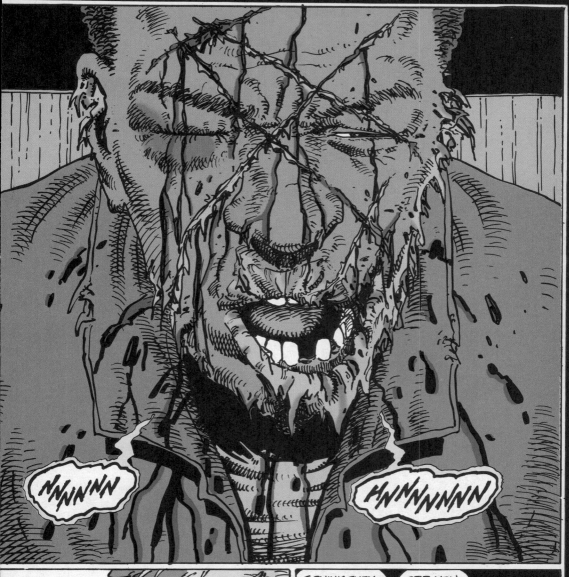

NNNNN

HNNNNNN

AW NO! AW BLOODY HELL, NO!!

I THINK THEY WANT TO BE ALONE...

SEE YOU LATER...

DEEEZZ!!

DUNNO. WASN'T HERE AT LUNCH.

WELL, IS THERE SOMEONE WHO WAS? IT'S *IMPORTANT*...

CAROL WAG. LEAVE HER 'TIL SHE'S NOT SO BUSY, RIGHT?

RIGHT, RIGHT...

CAROL! HEY, CAROL, YOU SEEN ME BROTHER?

HELLO, GEORGE!

DEZ, INNIT? HE WAS HERE WITH JOHN WOZZNAME, JUST AFTER LUNCH. WHAT'S WRONG, ANY-WAY?

HE WAS MEANT TO BE HOME AT *TWO*--ME MUM'S WORRIED *SICK*, Y'KNOW?

NOT SURPRISED, IF HE'S OUT WITH JOHN CONSTANTINE.

WHAT... WHAT D'YOU MEAN?

BLOKE'S BAD LUCK, INNE? FRIGGIN' JONAH...

MARTIN!

WELL, HE IS. WHAT ABOUT THAT RITCHIE SIMPSON, eh? CONSTANTINE'S MATE? BURNT TO A CRISP DOWN THE FACTORY...AN' THAT NUN HE USED TO HANG ABOUT WITH--THEY FOUND HER HEAD SPIKED AT THE TOP'VE THEM BLOODY STAIRS AT MORNINGTON CRESCENT...

THANK YOU, MARTIN.

LOOK, GEORGE, JOHN'S ALL RIGHT, OKAY? AND I'M SURE DEZ IS FINE TOO...

CAROL, IS THAT BATES LAD STILL LIVING IN KILBURN?..

OH, HE'S BAD NEWS, GEORGE...

BATESEY? GEORGE FOSTER, REMEMBER?

YEAH, I KNOW YOU STILL OWE ME ONE.

YOU STILL LOOKING AFTER THAT SAWN-OFF FOR JOE HOLLIS?

YEAH? EVEN BETTER.

I NEED IT.

ALL DAY THEY TALKED, AND WHEN TWILIGHT CAME THEY WANDERED UNDER SKIES OF DEEPEST, DARKEST BLUE...

THEY LOOKED FOR ALL THE WORLD LIKE LOVERS.

GABRIEL KNEW IT, TOO. THOSE EYES THAT SPARKLED FULL OF GOODNESS, THE LIPS THAT SPREAD INTO DELIGHTED SMILES...

THE LIFE AND JOY AND TRUTH AND PURITY...

OH FATHER, REJOICE.

WHATEVER IT WAS YOU WANTED THEM TO BE... THIS GIRL IS IT.

ARE THESE CHERRY TREES?

I BELIEVE SO, JULIE. THEY ARE.

I LOVE THEM IN THE SPRING, DON'T YOU? WITH THE BLOSSOM?

I THINK I'M HAPPIEST IN SPRING.

WHAT COULD IT HURT?

NO GUILT, GABRIEL.

THE WEIGHT SLIPPED FROM HIS SHOULDERS, AT LONG LAST...

NO GUILT.

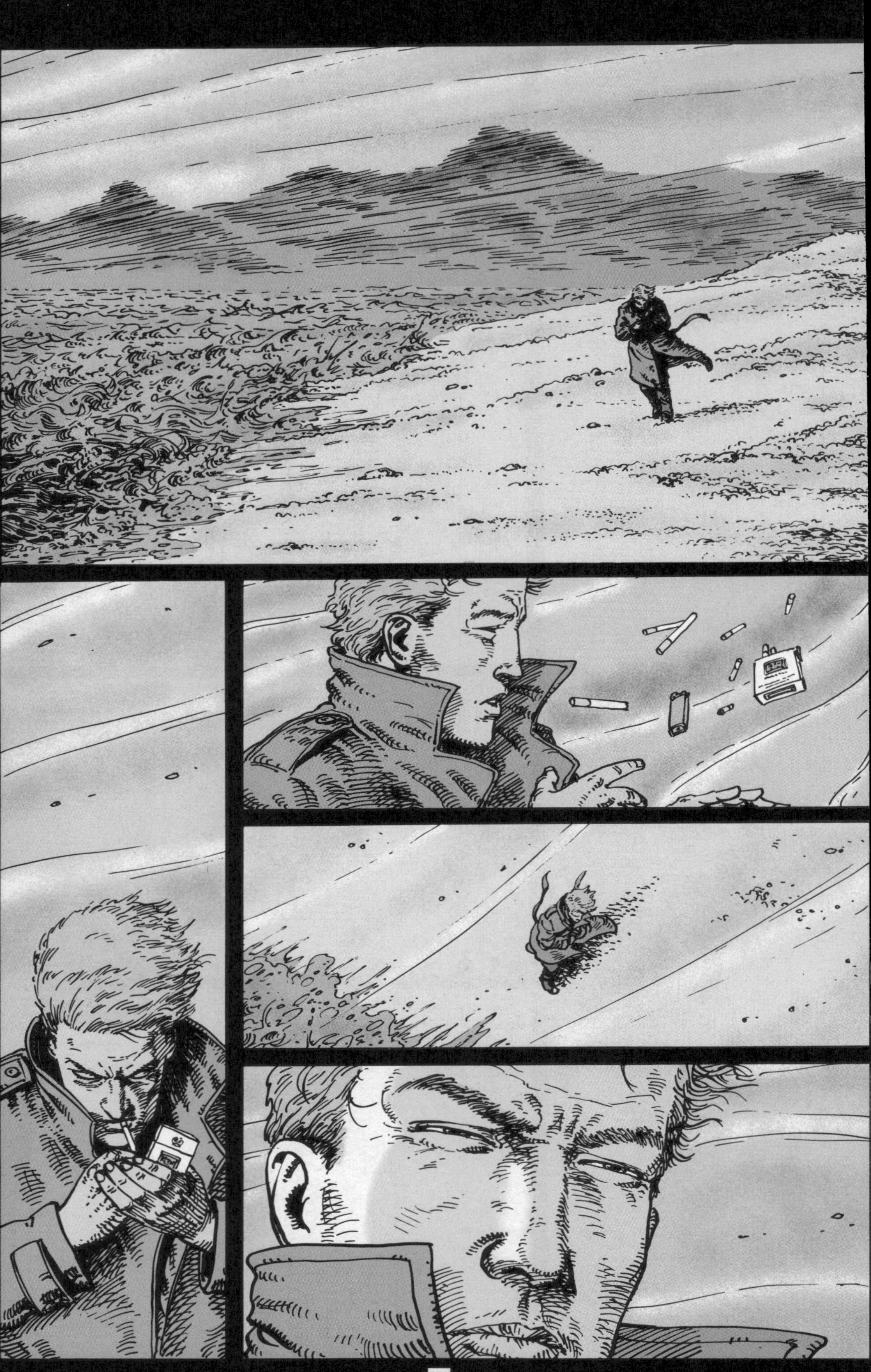

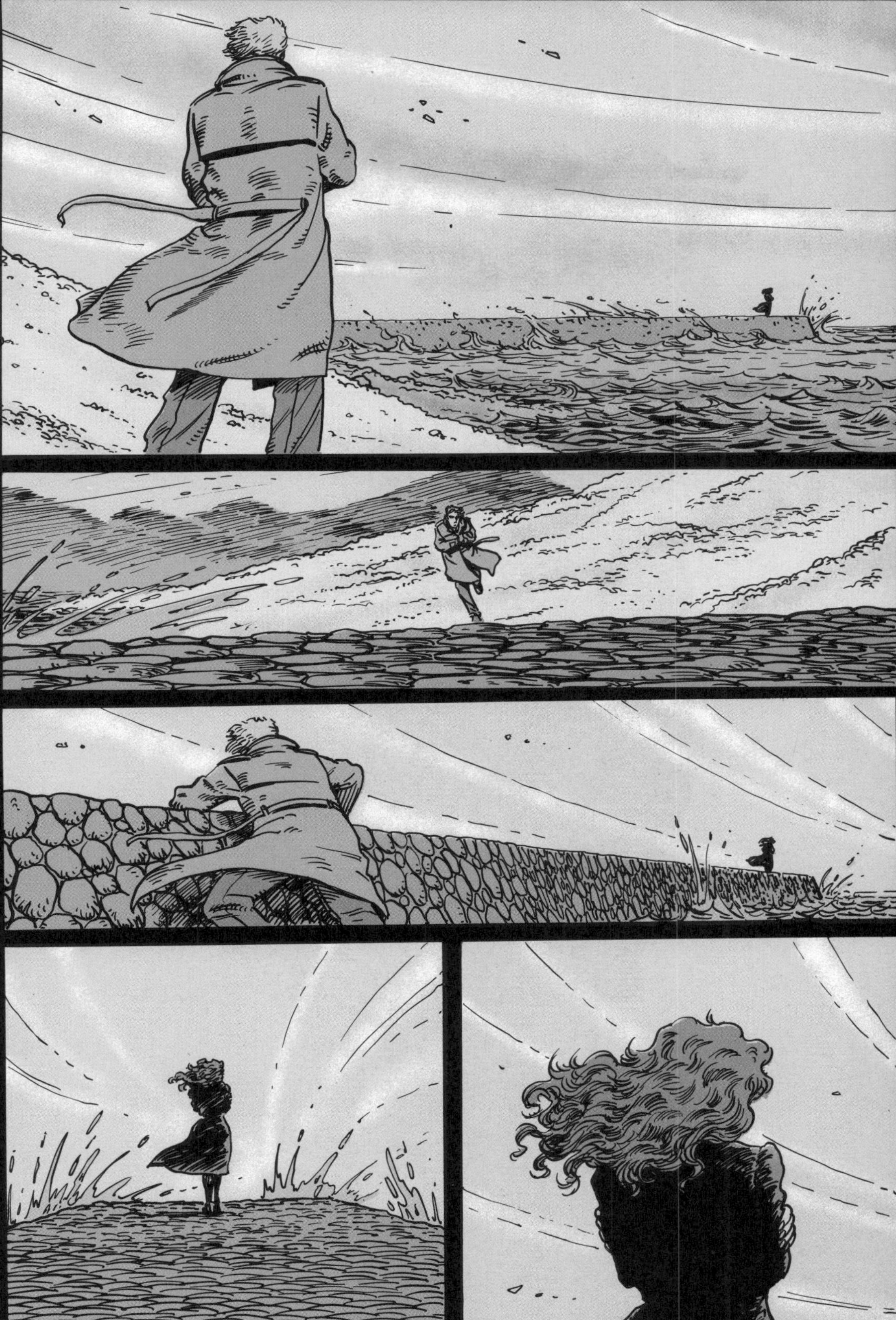

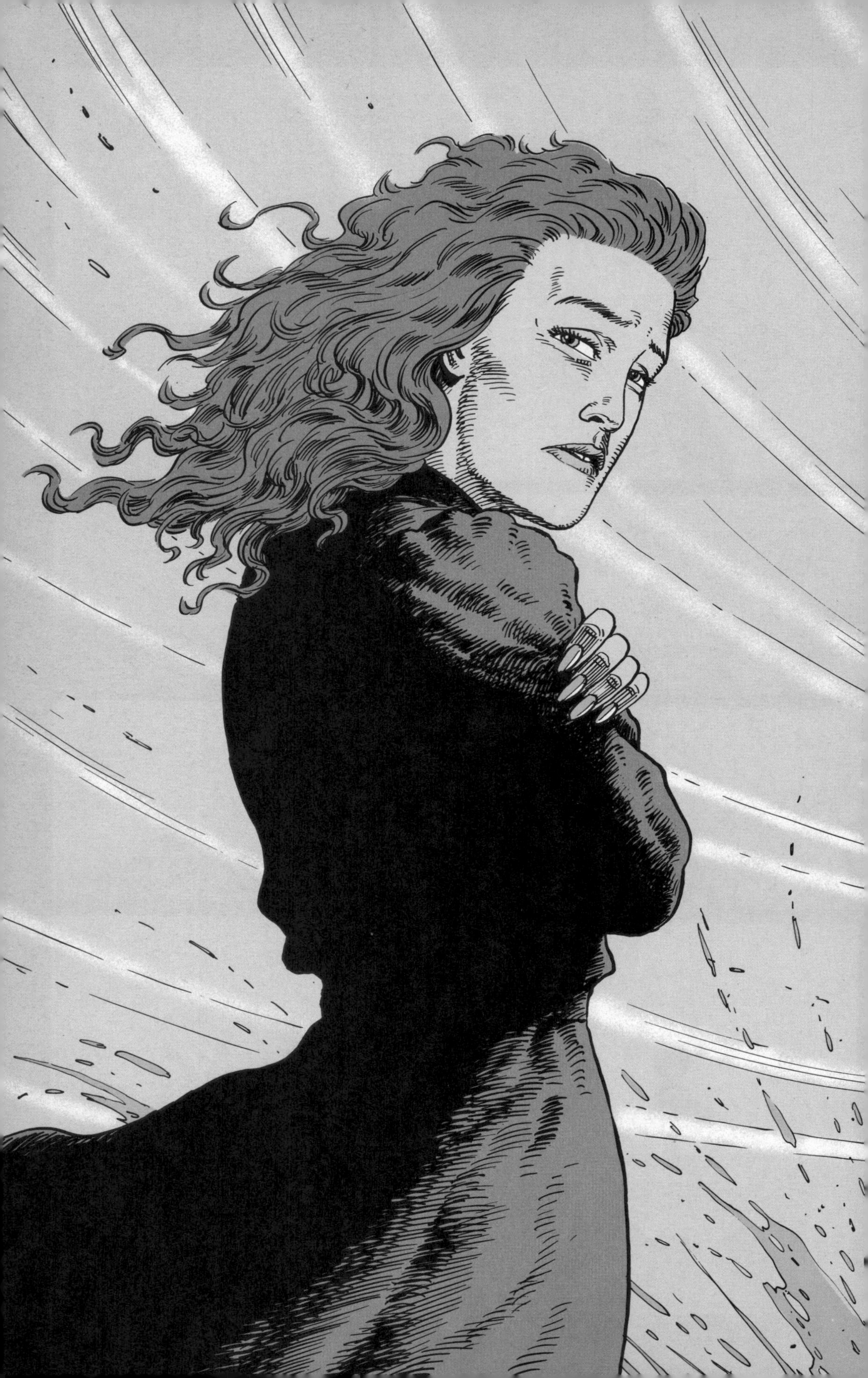

KIT.

NEXT:
GOD HELP
THE GUILTY

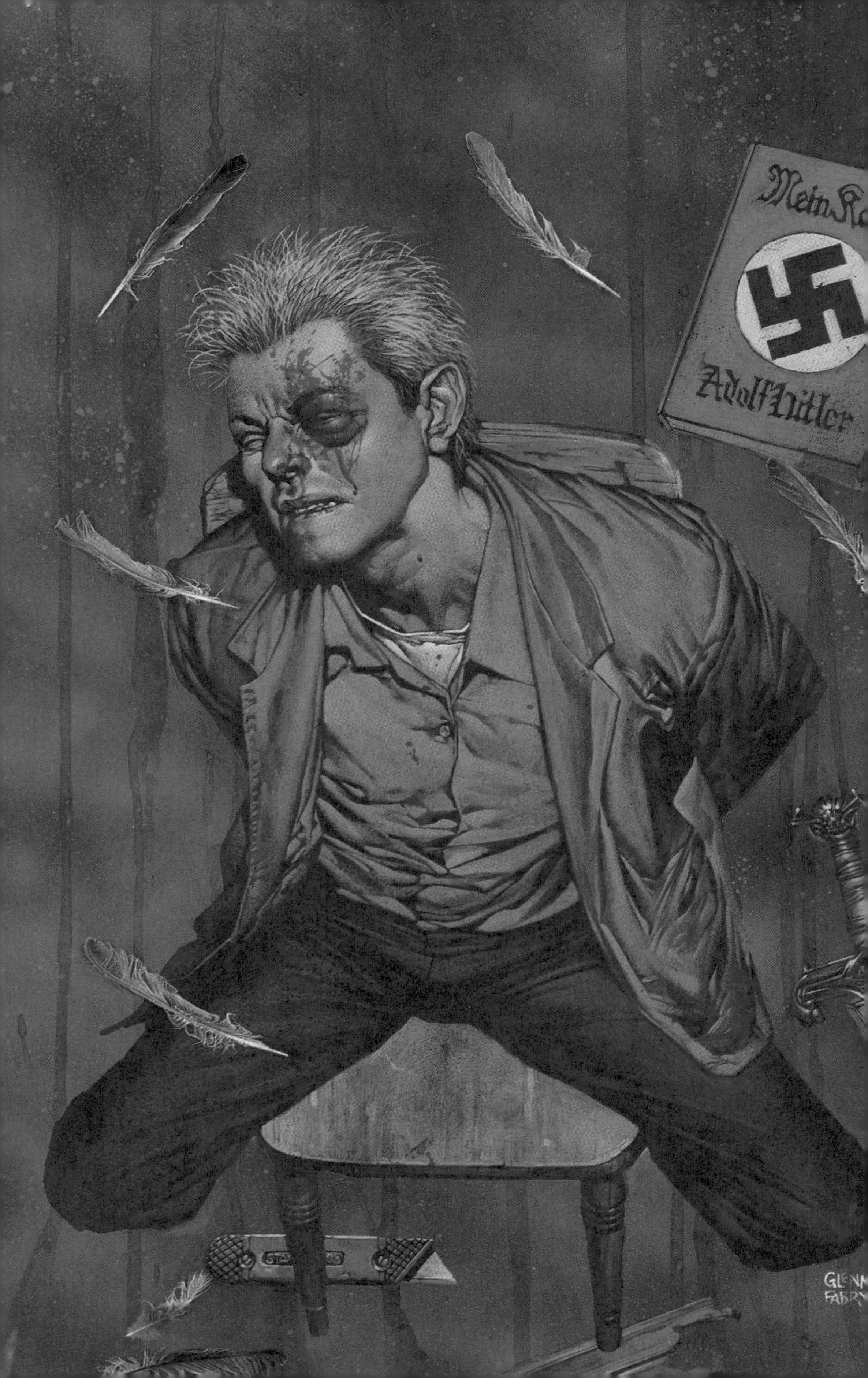
Adolf Hitler
GLENN FABRY

DEZ DIED AN HOUR AGO.

HE COULDN'T BREATHE WITH HIS THROAT CRUSHED, AND ALL I HEARD WAS A SOFT LITTLE HISS OF A RATTLE, SLIDING OUT FROM THE BUTCHER'S SHOP THAT USED TO BE HIS MOUTH.

SORRY, OLD SON. I'LL SEE YOU SOON.

AND KIT... SOMETHING'S HAPPENED TO HER, AND I CAN'T DO A THING.

I'VE LET HER DOWN.

I ALWAYS KNEW I WOULD.

YOU FROM ROOM SERVICE?

FEAR and LOATHING PART THREE
DOWN TO EARTH

GARTH ENNIS • writer STEVE DILLON • artist
TOM ZIUKO • colors gaspar • letters
STUART MOORE • editor

COME ON IN. I DON'T BITE, YOU KNOW!

I-I AM FINE...

WELL, IT'S NOT MUCH, BUT IT'S HOME...

GABRIEL... D'YOU MIND IF I ASK YOU...?

IS THIS YOUR FIRST TIME?

OH NO!

I MEAN, NOT LIKE THIS, OR, OR--

YES.

IT'S OKAY.

WHY WAS THE COON CARRYING ALL THE LITERATURE? SEVERAL COPIES OF THE NEWSPAPER, OUR POSTERS... KNOW YOUR ENEMY, IS THAT IT?

OR ARE YOU UP TO SOMETHING?

DOESN'T MATTER.

YOU THINK I'M A STUPID MAN, DON'T YOU?

I MEAN, OBVIOUSLY I'M NOT. I HIT YOU AS SOON AS YOU WENT NEAR THE ANGEL, BUT...

IT'S NICE TO HAVE SOMEONE TO LOOK DOWN ON, ISN'T IT?

BUT ALL THE SAME, YOU PROBABLY THINK: "PATTERSON? THAT LITTLE SHIT? I COULD HAVE HIM FOR BREAKFAST. HE'S JUST SOME TOSSER GOT CHUCKED OUT OF PUBLIC SCHOOL, NO BETTER THAN THE ARSE-HOLES HE'S IN CHARGE OF..."

BECAUSE WE'RE ALL SCARED, CONSTANTINE. WE'RE SCARED OF LOSING THE LITTLE WORLDS WE'VE HACKED OUT FOR OUR- SELVES, AND IF WE SEE SOME- ONE TRYING TO TAKE THEM AWAY FROM US...

THAT'S GREAT. WE DON'T HAVE TO BE SCARED ANYMORE.

WE CAN HATE.

THAT'S WHERE I COME IN, YOU SEE.

"LOOK AT THOSE BLOODY NIGGERS," I SAY. "LOOK AT THEM COMING OVER HERE LIKE THEY OWN THE PLACE, TAKING OUR JOBS, SCREWING OUR WOMEN... FRIGGING PAKIS TAKING OUR BUSINESSES AWAY..."

WORKS A TREAT.

OF COURSE, THE LIBERALS MAKE THEIR FILMS AND SO ON--SEARING INDICTMENTS OF THE STUPIDITY OF RACISM, WITH CLEVER PLOTS AND METAPHORS THAT DRIP WITH INSIGHT... AND PEOPLE SAY "YES! IT IS WRONG TO HATE A MAN FOR THE COLOR OF HIS SKIN!"

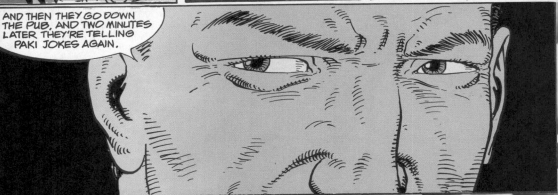

AND THEN THEY GO DOWN THE PUB, AND TWO MINUTES LATER THEY'RE TELLING PAKI JOKES AGAIN.

THAT'S YOUR PROBLEM, REALLY. AVERAGE LEFTY JUST DOESN'T REALIZE-- THEY'RE ASKING PEOPLE TO ACT AGAINST THEIR *INSTINCTS*.

NOT ME. *BE SCARED*. GO *AHEAD* AND HATE.

HATE ENOUGH, AND YOU'LL FORGET YOU LIVE IN A SHITHOLE WITH NO JOB, NO HEALTH SERVICE AND NO SECURITY, AND YOU'RE A FRIGGING MORON WITH NO HOPE OF ANYTHING.

AND WE'VE *GOT* TO KEEP THE MORONS OCCUPIED, HAVEN'T WE?

YOU KNOW SOMETHING, CHARLIE?

WHEN YOU GLOAT, YOU DO IT IN STYLE.

YOU TALK TOO LOUD IN THE FRIGGIN' *PUB*, ARSEHOLE-- YOU AN' THOSE NAZIS DOWN THE KING'S HEAD! WHERE YOU GOT 'EM?

WH-WHAT? COME *ON*, MATE! *PLEASE!*

"SO WE GOT 'EM, RIGHT? CONSTANTINE AN' 'IS BLOODY MONKEY! FRIG THE BOTH'VE 'EM!"

I'VE BEEN UP ALL NIGHT LOOKIN' AN I WANT ME *BROTHER!* *WHERE?!*

PUTNEY! OLD FIELD OFF THE TRACKS, IN THIS SHED AT THE BOTTOM! I SWEAR!

RIGHT...

DON'T KILL ME!

RELAX.

YOU NEVER TOLD ME, FATHER

DIDN'T KNOW

COULD NEVER HAVE DREAMED

SHE'S

SHE FEELS LIKE

HEAVEN

FATHER

OH MY FATHER

WHAT SHE DOES

GABRIEL?

WITH HER FINGERS--

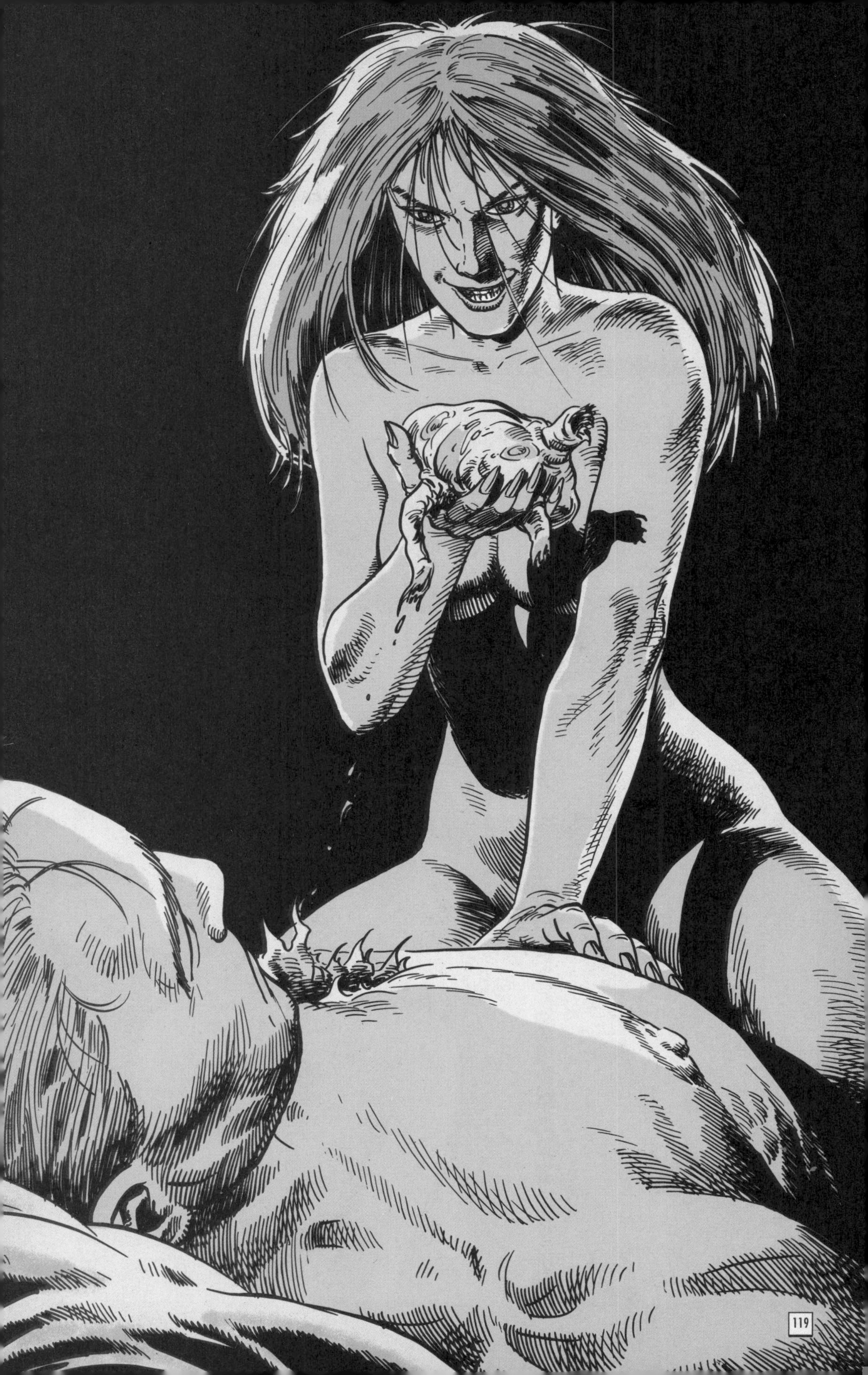

LIKE THAT?

YOU BETTER GO NOW, GABRIEL.

YOUR *DADDY* WANTS A WORD.

GOT YOU, YOU BASTARD.

ALL RIGHT, CHARLIE-- WHY DON'T YOU STICK YOUR SPEECHES BACK UP YOUR ARSE AND TELL ME WHAT YOU WANT WITH THE SNOB?

eh? HOLD ON A MINUTE, BOYS.

I'M SURPRISED YOU HAVE TO ASK...

YOU KNOW THIS COUNTRY'S GOING TO TURN NASTY IN A FEW YEARS, CONSTANTINE. YOU CAN SEE THE WAY IT'S HEADING...

I MAY NOT BE AN EXPERT ON MAGIC, BUT I KNOW IT HELPS TO HAVE SOME MYSTIC CLOUT IN AFFAIRS OF STATE.

AND YOU CAN'T CLOUT MUCH HARDER THAN A FALLEN ARCHANGEL, CAN YOU?

WELL...

CHARLIE, YOU HAVEN'T A HOPE OF CORRUPTING HIM. HOW WERE YOU GONNA DO IT? GET HIM TO SAY THE LORD'S PRAYER BACKWARDS?

YOU'RE TOO LATE, ANYWAY. I'VE DONE IT. HE FELL TONIGHT.

SO YOU UNTIE ME, AND FETCH ME SILK CUT...

AND I'LL GIVE HIM TO YOU ON A PLATE.

121

UH...YOU LOT DUMP HIM, OKAY? I'LL BE IN TOUCH.

IF THIS IS A WIND-UP--!

GROW UP.

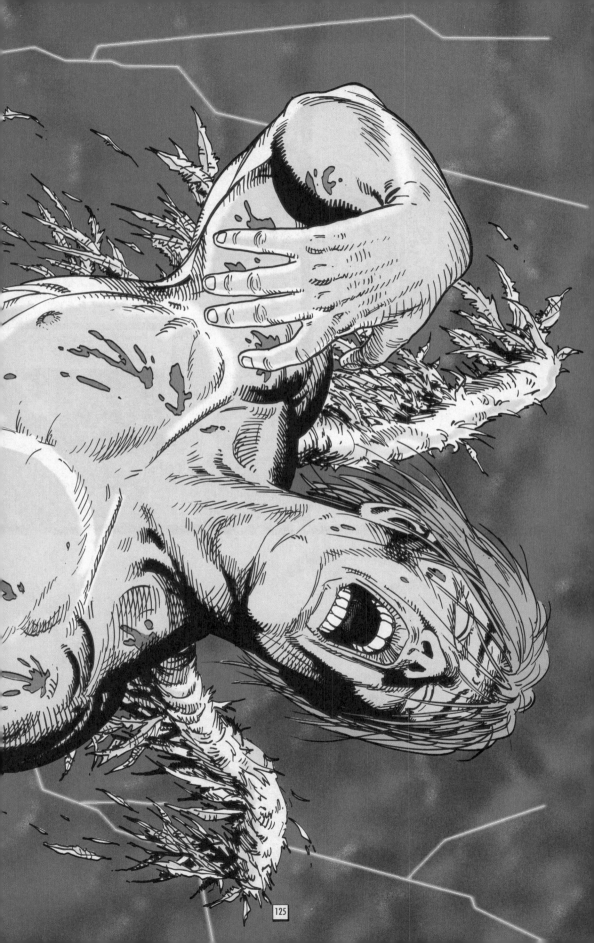

...BUT WHY DID YOU SCREW HIM UP? WHAT DID YOU WANT WITH HIM?

NONE OF YOUR BUSINESS.

I'LL GET WHAT I WANT FROM HIM, THEN HE'S YOURS. THAT'S ALL YOU NEED TO KNOW.

AND YOU'LL BE LUCKY IF YOU GET TUPPENCE, YOU FAT LITTLE BASTARD...

YOU'RE GOING DOWN, CHARLIE. YOU AND AS MANY OF THOSE BOOTBOYS OF YOURS AS I CAN MANAGE. AND IF KIT'S HURT--

...IF KIT'S HURT, CHARLIE, I'LL LEAVE YOU ALIVE WHEN I'M FINISHED.

BADAMM

HHHHHH

GEORGE?

FOR CHRIST'S SAKE--!

I SAW THEM PUTTIN' DEZ IN THE CAR, RIGHT? THEY FRIGGIN' KILLED HIM!

I KNOW, SON. I SAW HIM TOO.

BUT I HAD THIS BASTARD EATING OUT'VE ME HAND, THERE. I WAS GONNA TAKE HIM AND HIS WHOLE PACK OF BASTARDS TO PIECES...

SCREW YOU, CONSTANTINE.

BADAMM

DON'T YOU *EVER* FRIGGIN' JUDGE ME.

AH, SHIT.

NO, I DIDN'T TELL THE POLICE! D'YOU THINK I'M BLOODY STUPID OR SOMETHIN'?

JESUS, ALL RIGHT, LUV... WHERE'D YOU STAY?

CHAS'S SOFA. ONCE I REALIZED *YOU* WEREN'T BOTHERIN' YOUR ARSE TO TURN UP--

IT WAS TIED TO A CHAIR WITH THE REST OF ME.

YOU PROMISED TO LEAVE ME OUT'VE IT, JOHN. THAT'S THE ARRANGEMENT, REMEMBER?

AW, DON'T BE CLEVER.

YEAH.

SHIT. LOOK, LUV-- I'VE GOT TO NIP OUT FOR A BIT, RIGHT?

AYE.

BUT BEFORE YOU NIP ANYWHERE YOU CAN GET IN THE KITCHEN AND CLEAN UP ALL THAT FRIGGIN' SHITE!!

MUST BE GETTING SOFT. ANYONE ELSE GAVE ME A BOLLOCKING LIKE KIT DID THIS MORNING, I'D'VE JUST PISSED OFF ON 'EM...

HAVE TO SMOOTH HER OVER LATER.

BIT OF CROWING TO DO NOW.

ELLIE?

THAT'S ME.

ANY TROUBLE?

EASY-PEASY. SMELT HIM A MILE OFF.

SHOP AT SPAR

DID HE DO THE CHERRY BLOSSOM?

YEAH, YOU WERE RIGHT. THE BIG SOPPY GIT...

FIVER YOU OWE ME.

I'M IN TROUBLE WITH YOUR OPPOSITION, REMEMBER? YOU WOULDN'T HELP ME BEFORE. HAD TO FIX IT ME OWN WAY. PISSED 'EM OFF.

AS FOR ME, I JUST WANTED TO SEE YOU SCREWED.

WHY?

SHOP AT SPAR

YOU'RE ME NEW MINDER.

I AM NOTHING OF YOURS, CONSTANTINE. THAT SHRED OF PRIDE-- IT'S ALL I HAVE LEFT, NOW.

THIS IS THE ONLY THING KEEPING YOUR ARSE OUT OF THE FIRE.

SHOP AT SPAR

CHRIST, I HATE BEING THE BEARER OF BAD NEWS.

BEEN DOING ME HOMEWORK, GABE. ACCORDING TO A LITTLE BOOK I BOUGHT RECENTLY...

WANT ME TO SQUASH IT, *eh*?

COME ON, GABRIEL! IF YOU'RE GONNA FALL, YOU MIGHT AS WELL GO ALL THE WAY!

YOU'LL NEVER UNDERSTAND WHAT YOU'VE TAKEN FROM ME...

NOW YOU KNOW HOW IT FEELS.

YOU KILLED MY LOVER, YOU ARROGANT BASTARD. HE WAS AN ANGEL--BUT YOU DIDN'T BLOODY CARE WHAT YOU WERE TAKING FROM *HIM*, DID YOU?

NO.

BUT CONSTANTINE, I CAN SEE YOU'RE NOT JUST LOOKING FOR PROTECTION.

WHY IS IT... WHEN PEOPLE LIKE YOU SEE SOMETHING PURE AND GOOD AND BEAUTIFUL...

THAT YOU HAVE TO KICK IT DOWN AND DRAG IT THROUGH THE MUD?

ANYWAY, ENJOYABLE AS ALL THIS IS...

IF YOU'RE GONNA BE WORKING FOR ME YOU'LL HAVE TO SMARTEN UP A BIT. THOSE WINGS STICK OUT A BLOODY *MILE*, MATE.

IF YOU HAVE TO ASK, YOU'LL NEVER KNOW.

NOT TO WORRY, THOUGH...

YOU JUST LEAVE IT TO YOUR UNCLE JOHN.

AT THE END OF IT, HE ASKED CONSTANTINE HOW HE'D BE SURE HIS HEART WAS SAFE. AND CONSTANTINE TURNED TO HIM, AND SMILED A SMILE HE'D BE SEEING IN HIS NIGHTMARES...

"TRUST ME."

NO MORE SNOB, THEN. NO MORE PRIDE.

JUST A FRIGHTENED, FALLEN ANGEL...

LYING IN THE DIRT.

THE END

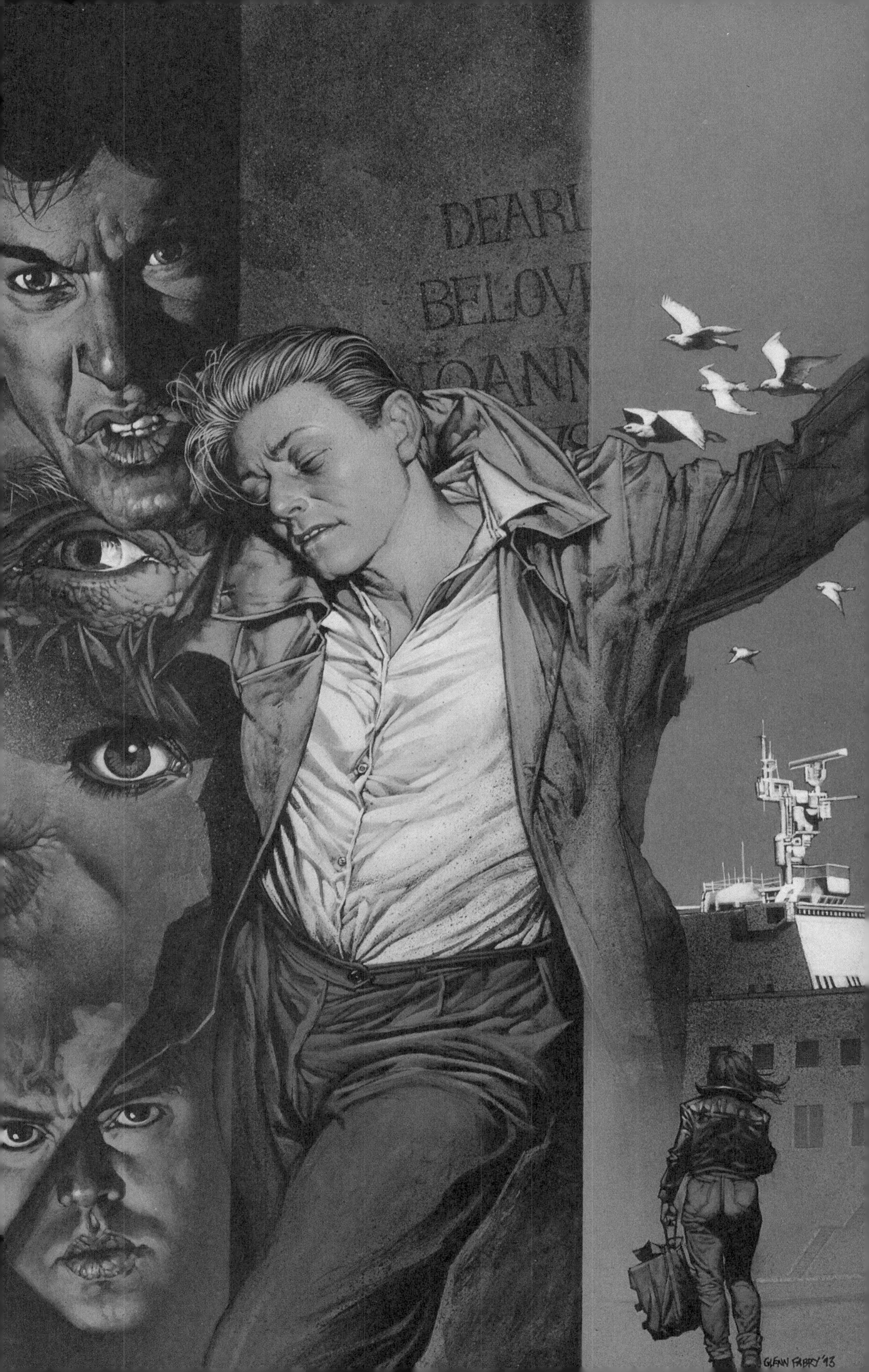
GLENN FABRY '93

D'YOU KNOW THE BEST WAY TO KILL A MAN?

TO MAKE IT HURT THE MOST?

TO TWIST THE KNIFE IN HIS HEART AND SOUL, AND LAUGH WHEN HE SCREAMS AND DIES?

YOU PUT THE BLADE IN HIS BEST FRIEND'S HAND...

AND YOU KILL THE POOR BUGGER WITH LOVE.

END OF THE LINE

GARTH ENNIS • *writer*   STEVE DILLON • *artist*   TOM ZIUKO • *colors*
TODD KLEIN • *letters*   JULIE ROTTENBERG • *assistant editor*   STUART MOORE • *editor*

SHE WAS NERVOUS.

SHE COULD'VE WRITTEN HIM A LETTER, BUT THAT WAS A STUPID WEE GIRL'S THING TO DO, AND SHE HATED CHICKENING OUT OF ANYTHING....

GOD, THOUGH, THIS WAS GONNA DESTROY HIM. SHE'D SEEN ENOUGH OF THE REAL HIM TO KNOW THAT.

TYPICAL....!

AYE, RIGHT ENOUGH. MEN WOULD TAKE YOU FOR GRANTED, COME TO RELY ON YOU--YOU'D BE LIKE A FRIGGIN' FOUNDATION HOLDIN' THEM UP, HALF THE TIME--

BIG BLOODY KIDS.

BUT ALL THE SAME....

ALL RIGHT?

HIYA.

YOU'RE TALKING TO ME AGAIN, THEN. 'BOUT BLOODY TIME...

I'M AWAY BACK TO BELFAST, JOHN.

FOR... FOR HOW LONG?

FOR GOOD.

I'M FED UP WITH THIS TOWN. IT SMELLS ROTTEN, SO IT DOES. AND THE PEOPLE CARRY ON LIKE -- I DUNNO. IT'S LIKE THEY'RE BEATEN. THEY'VE NOTHING LEFT IN THEM.

AND I DON'T WANT TO BE WITH YOU ANYMORE, JOHN.

I WANT TO GO HOME AND SEE ALL MY FRIENDS AGAIN, NOT JUST TALK TO THEM ON THE PHONE...

LOOK... I MEAN...

KIT...I KNOW THAT WAS ROUGH, THOSE TWO ARSEHOLES LAST WEEK--

YOU PROMISED NOT TO DO THAT STUFF ROUND ME, REMEMBER?

I DON'T WANT YOU TO BE PERFECT. I JUST WANT A QUIET LIFE WITHOUT SOME BASTARD KICKING MY DOOR DOWN AND COMING AT ME WITH A SWITCHBLADE.

YOU LET ME DOWN.

YEAH, BUT YOU KNOW WHAT I GET UP TO! YOU CAN'T EXPECT TO BE LEFT OUT OF IT FOREVER!

BUT I DIDN'T EVEN KNOW ABOUT THEM!

NOBODY'S PERFECT, LUV...

A QUIET LIFE? SO YOU'RE MOVING TO BELFAST?

OH, DON'T BE SO BLOODY STUPID!

140

YOU'VE NEVER EVEN BEEN THERE. YOU DON'T KNOW WHAT YOU'RE TALKIN' ABOUT.

KIT, THIS IS--PLEASE, LUV, I THOUGHT WE--

I'VE NEVER GOT THIS CLOSE TO ANYONE BEFORE, RIGHT? *NEVER.* I'VE NEVER FELT SO *GOOD*, EITHER. AND I DEFINITELY NEVER SAID STUFF LIKE THIS TO ANYONE IN MY *LIFE.*

I...

AND NOW YOU'VE RUINED IT ALL, JOHN.

BLOODY HELL...

HOW DID YOU GET TO BE SO *COLD*?

I'M NOT FRIGGIN' COLD! JUST 'CAUSE YOU'VE MADE A BALLACKS OF YOUR LIFE AN' YOU'VE GOT A HEAD FULL'VE MAD DOG'S SHITE, DOESN'T MEAN EVERYONE ELSE HAS!

RIGHT?!

YOU'RE A STUPID, SELFISH BASTARD, JOHN. AND YOU'VE NEVER REALLY CARED ABOUT ANYONE.

I'M GETTING THE TRAIN AT HALF THREE. THE RENT'S PAID 'TIL THE END OF THE WEEK--YOU CAN STAY HERE 'TIL THEN IF YOU WANT.

PISS OFF.

142

OI! CONSTANTINE!

YOU CAN TAKE YOUR BLOODY OUL' SHITE WITH YOU!

YOU PISS OFF!

JESUS!

THE DUKE OF

THAT'S IT.

THAT CAN'T BE IT.
SHE CAN'T JUST--

THAT'S IT.

CAN'T BE IT.

A DREAM.

STILL THERE IN BED
BESIDE HER. NOT HERE
WITH NINE PINTS IN ME,
I'M WITH HER.

WAKE UP
ANY SECOND.

WAKE UP.

THAT'S

IT

OH JESUS...!

IT'S LIKE THE GROUND'S GONE FROM UNDER ME FEET, FOR CHRIST'S SAKE--

HAVE TO KEEP A GRIP. I'LL GO TO BITS, CHRIST, SHE CAN'T BE GONE!

THIS IS GONNA KILL ME IF I DON'T WISE UP--I'M NOT GONNA CRY, AM I?

NO! DON'T LOSE IT!

EXCEPT I DON'T THINK I CARE ANYMORE ...

KIIIITT...

SAD BASTARD.

WHAT'D YOU SAY?

UH...

SHIT!

DID YOU CALL ME SAD? I'LL FRIGGIN' SMACK YOU ONE, YOU LITTLE TURD!

WAS IT YOU, THEN?

I-- I--

LOOK, PISS OFF, MATE, WILL YOU? IT WASN'T ME--

IT WAS!

YOU LITTLE BASTARD! YOU'RE CALLIN' ME SAD? YOU'RE SAD, YOU MOP-HEADED WANKER!

GET OFF ME! GET OFF!

LEAVE HIM ALONE, RIGHT?

ARSEHOLE!

146

MY FRIGGIN' FACE--

JESUS!

NO! LEAVE ME ALONE!

YOU PATHETIC LITTLE SHIT! USED TO BE KIDS HAD A BIT OF FIRE IN 'EM--YOU BASTARDS'RE JUST SMARTARSES, E'D OUT OF YOUR SKULLS HALF THE TIME!

NO BLOODY USE TO ANYONE, ARE YOU?!

PLEASE, PLEASE--

HERE! YOU! STOP THAT!

GET LOST, YOU WITCH!

DON'T YOU TALK TO ME LIKE THAT! I'LL HAVE YOU BARRED! I'LL GET MY TOM ON YOU!

SEEING WE'RE TALKING ABOUT SAD, SUNSHINE--WHAT ABOUT YOU TOUCHING UP YOUR KID SISTER IN HER PRAM?

HUH...HUH... HOW DID...?

I KNOW.

JESUS... CHRIST...

CURIOUS, WERE YOU? OR CAN YOU JUST NOT FIND A GIRL YOUR OWN AGE?

AFTER ALL, SHE'S ONLY SIX MONTHS OLD. SHE WON'T REMEMBER, WILL SHE?

BLOODY MARVELOUS.

'ERE! SOME TOERAG OUTSIDE'S STARTIN' A FIGHT! HE CALLED ME A BLOODY WITCH, HE DID!

EH?

JOHN...?

YOU'D ALL BE BLOODY DEAD IF IT WASN'T FOR ME-- AND THIS IS WHAT I DO IT FOR, IS IT? A PACK OF TOSSERS!

WHAT'S HE ON ABOUT?

AND IF IT'S NOT THE TOSSERS--

--IT'S THE BASTARDS!!

JOHN!

JOHN! FOR FRIG'S SAKE, MATE!

WHUH--?

RIGHT, WHAT THE BLOODY 'ELL'S ALL THIS? WHO CALLED MY ANGIE A WITCH?

AH, SHIT...

BLOKE'S JUST HAD A FEW, OKAY, MATE? I'M TAKING HIM HOME NOW, RIGHT?

HE'S A BLOODY LUNATIC! LOOK WHAT HE DONE TO THESE KIDS -- AN' WHAT ABOUT MY WIFE, EH?

ALL RIGHT, ALL RIGHT...

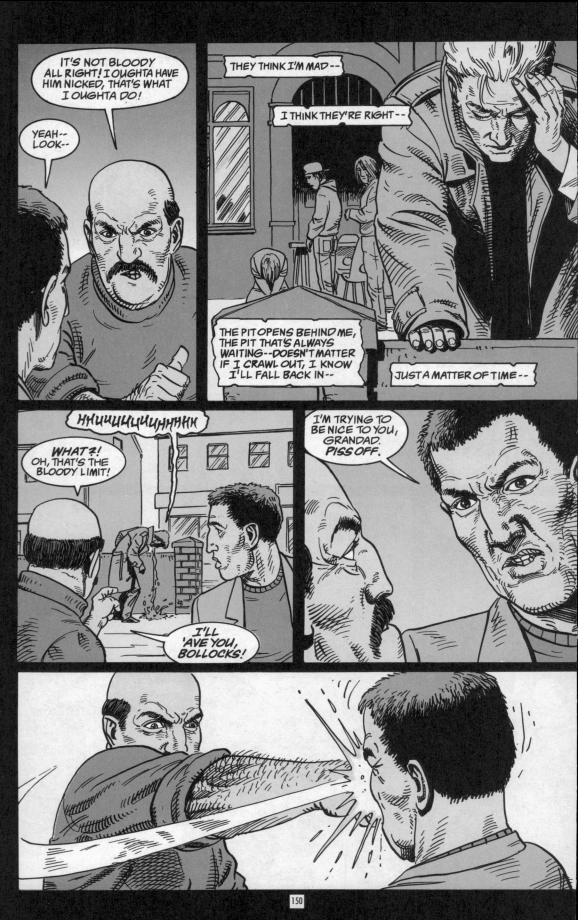

IT'S NOT BLOODY ALL RIGHT! I OUGHTA HAVE HIM NICKED, THAT'S WHAT I OUGHTA DO!

YEAH-- LOOK--

THEY THINK I'M MAD--

I THINK THEY'RE RIGHT--

THE PIT OPENS BEHIND ME, THE PIT THAT'S ALWAYS WAITING--DOESN'T MATTER IF I CRAWL OUT, I KNOW I'LL FALL BACK IN--

JUST A MATTER OF TIME--

KHUUUUЦЦUHHHHH

WHAT?! OH, THAT'S THE BLOODY LIMIT!

I'M TRYING TO BE NICE TO YOU, GRANDAD. PISS OFF.

I'LL 'AVE YOU, BOLLOCKS!

150

WELL?

COME ON, JOHN! WHAT WAS THAT ALL ABOUT?

LEAVE OFF, WILL YOU, CHAS?

NO, I BLOODY WON'T! YOU WERE BEIN' A RIGHT ARSEHOLE -- LIKE ONE OF THESE MAD OLD BASTARDS WHO RABBITS ON ABOUT NOT FIGHTING THE WAR FOR LAYABOUTS LIKE US, ALL THAT SHIT!

AND HAVE YOU SEEN THE FRIGGIN' STATE'VE MY FACE?

KIT LEFT ME.

OH SHIT.

THAT'S NOT SO BAD, IF SHE LET YOU STAY 'TIL FRIDAY.

RA-RA.

WELL, I'M SORRY ANYWAY.

MM.

RIGHT, I'LL SHUT ME MOUTH. I KNOW HOW YOU FEEL, LIKE...

CHAS, YOU DON'T HAVE A FRIGGIN' CLUE HOW I FEEL. WHAT WOULD YOU KNOW, LIVING WITH THAT FAT BITCH?

SO JUST SHUT UP, FOR GOD'S SAKE...

NOW JUST A BLOODY MINUTE--!

OH, BOLLOCKS... PISS OFF, WILL YOU, CHAS? GO BACK WHERE YOU BELONG, WITH ALL THE OTHER ARSEHOLES.

AAAWHH!!

HUUAH! WHA--

I'LL FRIGGIN' SHOW YOU WHERE *YOU* BELONG, CONSTANTINE!

AAHH!

AAAH! GET OFF! GET THE FRIG OFF ME!

OW!

CHAS, FOR CHRIST'S SAKE--

GAHHHHH CCHHLLHCH!

AAACCHH! FORFUGGCHH!

UNNNH

PRICK.

YOU'LL COME... CRAWLIN' BACK...

YOU... YOU ALWAYS DO...

THINK...IT'S...MIDNIGHT...

BEEN MARKING OFF THE HOURS WITH WHISKEY.

WHAT'D BRENDAN CALL IT?

BOTTLED SUNSHINE, THAT'S WHAT HE SAID.

DOESN'T LOOK LIKE SUNSHINE TO ME. SLOPS IN THE BOTTLE LIKE A WINO'S PISS, DARK AND SOUR AND ROTTEN...

FRIGGIN' SHIT!!

AH, JESUS...

JESUS...

GOOD JOB I'VE GOT ANOTHER ONE

GATE'S NO PROBLEM.

ALL YOU NEED IS TO *WANT* TO GET IN...

I WANT, ALL RIGHT.

THIS IS WHERE I BELONG.

S'WHERE ALL ME MATES HANG OUT...

YOU SAW WHAT I WAS, KIT. YOU SAW RIGHT THROUGH ME FRONT AND YOU LIKED ME ANYWAY.

SO I MADE ME PLANS, AND I WHEELED AND DEALED AND DID WHAT I DO, JUST SO'S I COULD BE WITH YOU...

SHOULDN'T'VE BOTHERED WITH ALL THAT STUFF. SHOULD'VE DROPPED IT AND GONE OFF WITH YOU.

BOLLOCKSED EVERYTHING, JUST 'COS I CAN'T HANDLE THAT CLOSENESS. 'COS I'M AFRAID OF A *WORD*...

JUST ONE LITTLE WORD...

L
O
V
E